ADVANCE PRAISE

"The world is not suffering from a cynicism shortage. In fact, more of the generous naivety described in Joshua's book is exactly what we need right now."

—Seth Godin, Author, *The Song of Significance*

"*Dare to Be Naive* is full of engaging stories, humor, and practical advice. For those who strive to take on the complex challenge of evolving company culture, it's like having a mentor by your side."

—Marissa Rodgerson, Head of Innovation Strategic Design and Research, Wells Fargo

"Behavior change is hard because we're often in the dark about what makes us tick. *Dare to Be Naive* provides a simple framework to help you discover the beliefs that shape your behavior and the behaviors of those around you."

—Aaron Dignan, Entrepreneur, Podcast Host, and Author of *Brave New Work*

"Our behaviors and beliefs power much of the success we experience in business and life. When we pause and create space to reflect on what we believe, we realize some of those beliefs are self-limiting. Through anecdotes and provocative business ideas, this book will help you create that space."

—Nir Eyal, *WSJ* Bestselling Author of *Indistractable* and *Hooked*

"*Dare to Be Naive* blew me away. Joshua's take on mission-driven leadership is inspirational and focuses on the importance of leading with empathy, compassion, and a clear sense of purpose. The book is filled with practical advice and actionable steps that any leader can implement immediately. I appreciated the real-life stories and examples of leaders who have successfully implemented these strategies. This is a resource for anyone who wants to improve their leadership skills and create a more positive and purposeful workplace culture. Enjoy the ride!"

—McKell Purnell, VP Human Capital,
Omaha Public Power District

"Having worked with Joshua for several years, Joshua has stretched my own thinking, creativity, and introspection as a leader. Joshua is an innovator that cares about people and has a unique approach to solving problems and helping others. His insights are relevant to individual leaders as well as to teams."

—Eric Mooss, CEO, Bryan Medical Center

"The wise leader moves beyond 'either/or' thinking and begins to embrace more of the 'both/and.' Through compelling stories, business practices, and provocative questions, Joshua creates space for leaders to explore their emerging wisdom."

—Chip Conley, Hospitality Entrepreneur and
NYT Bestselling Author

"My initial inclination to the word *naive* is quite negative. I grew up in a rural area near a small community. People took care of each other. I was VERY naive—and later called out for it. After college and now years in business, I have become quite jaded. Trust does not come easy. After reading your book, I feel more equipped to identify beliefs that may be limiting, question them, and let my authenticity (maybe even naivete) into the room again. I'm looking forward to this journey of unlearning and choosing a path that leads to the new ROI (personally and professionally)."

—Peggy Christensen, Enterprise Software & Data Services Manager, Hamilton Telecommunications

"*Dare to Be Naive* gives you a shot of inspiration and just the right questions to help you think bigger about your life and business. I hadn't thought about many of the ideas Joshua brings up before I read this book, but I'm better for it."

—Diana Kander, *NYT* Bestselling Author and Keynote Speaker on curiosity and innovation

DARE
TO BE
NAIVE

DARE
TO BE
NAIVE

**HOW TO FIND
YOUR TRUE SELF
IN A NOISY WORLD**

Joshua Berry

IDEAPRESS
PUBLISHING

WASHINGTON, DC

IDEAPRESS
PUBLISHING

Printed in the United States

Ideapress Publishing | www.ideapresspublishing.com

All trademarks are the property of their respective companies.

Cover Design: Faceout Studio, Spencer Fuller
Interior Design: Jessica Angerstein

Cataloging-in-Publication Data is on file with the Library of Congress.

Hardcover ISBN: 978-1-64687-152-0

Special Sales
Ideapress books are available at a special discount for bulk purchases for sales promotions and premiums, or for use in corporate training programs. Special editions, including personalized covers, custom forewords, corporate imprints, and bonus content are also available.

1 2 3 4 5 6 7 8 9 10

To Chloe, Logan, Gavin, and Daphne—
May you always make space to listen to that authentic voice
inside of you. Go to the limits of your longing—the world
needs more of You in it.

Contents

Love says "I am everything."
Wisdom says "I am nothing."
Between the two, my life flows.

—NISARGADATTA MAHARAJ

Introduction

I dare you to be *more* naive.

Not willfully ignorant. Just more authentic and genuine, the original meaning of the word *naive*.

To dream bigger, be more curious, and focus more on what is possible in your life, in business, and in the world.

Many of the successful leaders I interviewed for this book used the phrase "this might sound naive . . ." and then proceeded to share an amazing idea, business practice, or truth.

If you are like them, you might fear being seen as naive. Maybe you use the word as a qualifier for some of your best ideas. In fact, you may have been told more than once in your life that you shouldn't be so naive.

Where did we learn this? What do we gain by holding this belief that we shouldn't be naive? And, more importantly, what do we lose?

I feared being seen as naive most of my life, at least in the negative sense of the word. I always wanted to be the smartest person in the room, and admittedly, there are times I still do. I would put on a mask and not share my true thoughts if they sounded outside of the mainstream. Any voice in my head that couldn't be backed up by a rational argument was shunned. I thought this was the way to truly be successful and was often rewarded for this behavior in family, work, and school.

Eventually, I learned that this fear of being naive was actually *preventing* me from having a greater impact in business and life.

LESSONS FROM THE PRODUCE AISLE

My first boss was a man named Craig. He was the store director of a large grocery retailer.

When I was sixteen, Craig promoted me to a supervisory position, well before I was ready and much younger than the corporate offices typically preferred. It was a bold move on his part, and I'm sure there were raised eyebrows at headquarters. Over the course of the next couple of years, Craig continued to spot and affirm my potential. He created the space for me to try new ideas and made it a safe place, even if I failed. I saw him invest in many other employees in similar ways.

Craig was always full of big, unconventional ideas on how to help the community. During my time working for him, I saw Craig champion citywide Easter egg hunts, community concerts, and countless scholarships, donations, and employment opportunities for the young and old alike. The ideas didn't always make immediate traditional business sense, and the main competitor in town thought Craig was naive. There were times he invited me to help, and I declined for fear of what others would think.

Craig had an interesting air about him. It was a mix of curiosity, energy, and wonderment, sprinkled with a sense of hope and optimism. Later in life, I eventually got the opportunity to ask Craig more about why he invested in me and others the way he did.

"I knew that taking care of the people who worked there, and taking care of the community, was the right thing to do. It just felt right. And often, if I took care of them, they'd take care of me."

He chose to be a little naive, and maybe that isn't always a bad thing. Craig set numerous company sales records and was eventually inducted into the company Hall of Fame not once, but twice. He consistently generated a strong return on investment while creating another ROI—Ripples of Impact—in the world.

I would go on to work at this grocery store chain for almost eight years, serving in a variety of management positions. Not every leader I met there embodied Craig's "it just felt right" view on people or community, but several did, and I've run into even more leaders like them over the last twenty-five years.

What causes leaders to invest in the growth of their people with such trust or faith? Why do they act this way? How do certain leaders naively "give first" to their customers, employees, or community with no promise it will be returned? And why are so many others reluctant to? What beliefs need to shift for more of these stories to happen in the first place?

In essence, what would happen if stories of successful, authentic leaders who created Ripples of Impact became the norm, not the exception?

Thankfully over the last two decades, including the last nine years as the cofounder and CEO of Econic, I've begun to hear these stories more and more. Our teams have helped numerous Fortune 500 companies with their culture, growth, and innovation efforts. I've assisted over one hundred start-up companies in understanding the basics of getting their businesses off the ground. And I've done this work in over twenty countries. Over the years, I'm seeing more of these Craig-like beliefs and stories become embedded in the systems and norms of organizations.

The result?

Traditional business growth and ROI, coupled with entire organizations actively showing concern for the care and growth of each other—concern for their employees, their communities, and the planet, regardless of if people perceive it as naive.

CHOOSE NAIVE

Most people think being naive, especially in business, is a bad thing. But based on my experiences, I've seen an intentional, *chosen* naivete lead to better business and a more fulfilled life. It is a return to elements of a childlike naivete rooted in something deeper we'll explore in this book. Beginning to admit what you don't know, setting your ego aside, and being open to the possibility that you're connected to others and this planet in a way that challenges logical explanation sounds more like emerging wisdom, not ignorance.

In this book, you'll learn why we fear being seen as naive and how to question that fear, especially so you can harness the positive attributes of a chosen naivete: curiosity, trust, authenticity, and optimism. Successful business leaders today need to develop a growth mindset and better emotional intelligence. This book will help you on that journey.

For those of you skeptical about a more conscientious, interconnected—and dare I say, heart-centered—approach to business, you are not alone. The current, industrial-age-inspired approaches to business have resulted in incredible gains in health, comfort, and prosperity for many people. That success should be honored and not torn down, but evolved.

We can't ignore the way most business is done today, especially in large corporations, which is creating an incredible burden on our environment and our society. Unfortunately, business leaders often fear being labeled as naive if they pursue social good while pursuing profits. And yet, we need leaders to lean into this chosen naivete to make the largest Ripples of Impact. Times are changing; *how* and *why* money is made is increasingly as important as *how much* money is made. More and more employees, customers, and business leaders agree.

Business has a major role in improving our society. According to a recent PwC study, 71 percent of large organizations are taking a good, hard look at how to evolve their business to do good while in pursuit of profit. Why? For some, they sound like

Craig—"it just feels right." For others, it's because consumers and employees are demanding it. And for the pure capitalists at heart, more and more organizations are proving, as you'll see in this book, how doing good *in* business is actually good *for* business.

In his 2018 letter to CEOs, BlackRock CEO Larry Fink observes that "society is demanding that companies . . . serve a social purpose," and argues that without such purpose, "no company . . . can achieve its full potential." The world's largest for-profit investor declared "to prosper over time, every company must not only deliver financial performance, but also show how it makes a positive contribution to society. Companies must benefit all of their stakeholders, including shareholders, employees, customers, and the communities in which they operate."

The world is always evolving, and so is how we lead. What follows is a carefully curated collection of stories I believe will inspire you just as they did me. For those of you who feel like you get mislabeled as naive because of your sense of trust, hope, and wonder, you will find peers and fellow business "rebels with a cause" in these stories.

WHAT TO EXPECT

The first chapter of this book will reintroduce you to the word naive and the history of its hijacking. You'll then learn the true story of a *reluctant* businessman and how his "naive" approach to business is changing the world. Next, you'll learn a simple approach to help you reflect on how your beliefs and those in business are evolving. If you're like me, you have limiting beliefs about yourself. Evolving those beliefs is key to less stress, more success, and greater Ripples of Impact in your work and personal life.

The second part of the book consists of short stories and examples of evolving, successful business practices some might call naive. Each chapter includes an invitation for you to practice reflection on the examples provided. I don't think you need another book telling you what new leadership traits you should *adopt*. Instead, I want to share with you an approach that gets you thinking critically and helps you *adapt*.

The end of the book will provide you with practical exercises on how to put new ideas and beliefs into action, inspired by my work with innovators and leaders in behavior change. It takes wisdom and courage to unlearn, relearn, and evolve, and I believe you have it in you to do this.

YOUR INVITATION

We need to reframe our idea of being naive, so consider this your invitation to reflect and act courageously. To be inspired by the stories and tactics of businesses and leaders who have chosen to prioritize things other than maximizing their own self-interest. Leaders who *don't* believe this is all just a zero-sum game. Leaders who are generating a different ROI—Ripples of Impact—and are still able to get a remarkable return on investment.

These are stories of leaders—probably like you—who see the evolution of business as one of the best shots we have at leaving a better world for our children and our children's children. Can you envision all of that good in business and people?

Dare to be naive with me.

Part 1

THE CONCEPT

It is not enough to be busy; so are the ants.
The question is: What are we busy about?

—Henry David Thoreau

Chapter 1

Naive: A Fresh Take on an Old Word

"What are you doing? You have to lock the car in this neighborhood! Are you naive?"

I had only been driving for a couple years, and this was my first real trip to the city. I was going to see a concert featuring the band Everclear. We had just parked at the Sokol Auditorium in an older neighborhood of Omaha, Nebraska. I turned to my friend, shrugged, and went back to lock the car.

Coming from a midwestern town of twenty thousand people, there were many times when my car sat unlocked. Either consciously or subconsciously, I was trusting that I was in a safe environment.

I don't know if it was my youth or my limited experiences or if it was just engrained in who I was. I think when we are younger, most of us are more trusting and less jaded.

We are more trusting of others, but also more trusting of ourselves and our untested abilities. This makes us more curious to try and learn, which for many people nurtures a virtuous cycle of safety, trust, and self-confidence.

As we grow up, we're often taught by those with more age and experience (or a louder microphone) that the world is less safe than we thought. And as such, that there is an expected way to do things, more mature and normal; that those who aren't like you should be approached with caution; and that veering even slightly off the beaten path—well, that's just naive. We are inundated with this message throughout our lives, and it becomes especially extreme in business.

"If you give those union workers an inch, they're going to take a mile."

"Make sure you get a contract signed with them and our lawyers are put on alert. We need to have a way to litigate this if it starts to go bad."

"This younger generation is lazy. They need more accountability and discipline."

"You just can't trust those people working from home. We need them back in the office so I can see they're actually working."

These are all statements I've heard in the past few years that highlight some common practices and beliefs in traditional businesses. At face value, these statements are neither blatantly nor absurdly false.

And yet, for many, encountering statements like these raises questions and doubts. But actually challenging these statements and ideas is another matter. Imagine yourself in a meeting with your peers or leaders, standing up to pronounce:

"Let's give the union workers as much as they say they need."

"Maybe we don't need a heavy contract with this group. I trust them."

"I was wrong. I think this younger generation just has different motivations than us."

"People working from home can be trusted, even if we can't walk by their desk and see them."

For some of you, that exercise might have been easy. Maybe you would have even taken some of those ideas further. For others, you wouldn't have dared to speak those thoughts, even if they popped into your mind. Others would judge you as too idealistic or optimistic, not fully rooted in "reality." Fear of being seen as naive or not in alignment with "the way we do things around here" are powerful demotivators. We've evolved as humans in a way that mostly favors those who stick with the tribe, who don't rock the boat.

I'm right there with you. For the longest time, being seen as "smart" was a core part of my identity that had been recognized and rewarded throughout my life. I worked hard at not being seen as naive.

For example, I used to have a habit of presenting my boldest, most "naive" ideas as someone else's, just to protect myself from the possibility that the idea might not be embraced as I'd hoped. Rather than outright claiming an opinion or idea, I would fabricate an opening like, "I heard someone say recently . . ." Speaking what I really believed felt at times unwise, especially when it came from a place others would deem as naivete.

And yet, here I am, advocating for exactly that. With the way the world continues to change and evolve, we unquestionably need more people willing to speak up and act on beliefs others might deem naive, idealistic, or unrealistically optimistic. By editing ourselves, we explicitly cut out the most special things any person has to offer—our unique insights synthesized from a lifetime of experience, our instinctive leaps of genius. By screening ourselves to present only the rational case accepted within the mainstream, we eliminate the option for transformational leaps.

One way to address this is by reexamining our relationship with the word *naive*. To start with, the meaning and usage of the word have evolved in a way that few of us realize, and that is not always to our benefit. More precisely, "It ain't what it used to be."

A RETURN TO NAIVETE

Today, the word *naive* is typically defined as "lacking worldly experience, wisdom, or judgment; unsophisticated." With that definition, it's easy to see why anyone would fear being labeled as naive. In English, we adopted the word directly from French in the late 1500s. And the French in turn adapted the word *naive* from the Latin word *nativus* a few centuries before that.

So, what did that root word originally imply? The Latin word *nativus* means "natural, native, imparted at birth." Other sources add descriptions of nativus like "not artificial, genuineness, authenticity."

The word *naive* didn't actually imply something negative until a few hundred years ago, well after it was already being used in English in a more neutral or positive way. In the seventeenth century, we see the first recorded uses of the word *naive* to imply someone as a fool or unsophisticated. This happens to coincide with the Age of Enlightenment, the Scientific Revolution, and shortly thereafter, the Industrial Age. In an era dominated by reason and colonialism, those who were "native" or not keeping up with the times were looked down upon. While the unfortunate evolution of the word makes sense, it does not serve us to dismiss intuitive, natural, or native wisdom.[1]

I know a lot of leaders today who are trying to be genuine, authentic, and not artificial. Yet they struggle to act on those things that just *feel* like the right thing to do. They stifle something innate—*nativus*. Yet when a thought arises that we're hesitant to speak aloud for fear of being judged as naive, we can't let go of that thought. Instead, we must consider whether it might be coming from a deeper wisdom, something that's been inside us from the start.

---

1 As I was sharing some of my findings with my friend Javier, he reminded me that the word for naive in Spanish is *ingenuo*. The Latin root *ingenuus* also refers to something native and "noble, upright, frank, candid, open; like a freeman" (Tufts University, n.d.) In ancient Rome, those freemen who were born free were *ingenui*. This is further confirmation that what was once seen as "naive" was that which was genuine, noble, not enslaved—a desirable characteristic.

MANAGING THE SPECTRUM

The *Oxford English Dictionary* describes naivete as an apparent or actual lack of experience and sophistication, often describing a neglect of pragmatism in favor of moral idealism. But we do not in fact need to choose between pragmatism and moral idealism. This is a false dichotomy. Instead, these are polarities or tensions to be managed. Think of it more like a spectrum.

What are the positives associated with being pragmatic? For starters, you might be seen as responsible, grounded, and reliable. If you take pragmatism to the extreme, where it starts to become cynical and pessimistic, you might encounter more of the negatives associated with it. You might miss out on real opportunities or feel more anxious or depressed than normal—even your overall health may suffer. In some studies, cynicism is linked to higher rates of heart disease and cancer-related deaths.

On the other side, what are the positives associated with being naive? It can lead to greater curiosity and ideas of what is possible. Being more genuine and authentic can result in less stress and feeling more grounded. But if you take naivete to the extreme, where it borders on ignorance, people manipulate your trust or gullibility and take advantage of you.

Where are you on this spectrum? And is it fixed, or could it shift?

When it comes to beliefs like this, there is no absolute right or wrong—just a spectrum to be managed. Any position you take along the spectrum will create gains and losses. In chapter 4, you'll learn a framework to help you with this.

Even though you're barely into this book, I'm betting you can already guess: I lean more toward the naive side of the spectrum. I believe you, dear reader, are innately good and worthy of trust. If the situation seems to suggest the opposite, I usually believe I need to squint a little better to see the good. Or I consider the conditions in life that have made those parts of you harder to find, but I know you're absolutely not a lost cause.

And I bring this perspective into practically every decision I make. I know I'm going to get taken advantage of 1 or 2 percent of the time. But in my experience, it makes the other 98 and 99 percent of life a lot better. Do I put my wallet out on the front doorstep every night? Nope. But do I do a lot of business off of just a handshake and provide a level of transparency to the people in our company that makes our accountants and my peers nervous? Yup.

"Wow, Josh, you really are naive. And we already read you grew up in a small midwestern town, so you're proving the point of the current definition of naivete: unworldly and unsophisticated."

"On the contrary," I retort. From what I can tell, I've led a pretty full life so far. I've visited or worked in over thirty countries, including living for extended periods of time in other cultures. I've lived in extravagant homes *and* in my grandparent's concrete-floored basement. I've had plenty of cash in the bank, *and* I know what it's like to live with government-assisted free lunches and food stamps. I've had tremendous business success *and* been cheated, lied to, and dragged into lawsuits. As a white male, I know I experience certain safeties and advantages, *and* I had an incarcerated parent during my early childhood, and I am a survivor of a deadly bus shooting. All that to say, I have plenty of reasons to trust others and life itself, *and* I have reasons to trust no one.

At the end of each day, I have a choice. When I make the space to truly, authentically listen to what my heart, mind, and gut are telling me, my choices tend to come across to others as a little naive.

But it's a *chosen* naivete.

There is a leader I admire named N. K. Chaudhary. He is the leader of Jaipur Rugs, one of the largest hand-knotted rug companies in the world that currently works with forty thousand artisans and sells in over sixty countries. Chaudhary has been called the "Gandhi of the carpet industry" and believes the core of the organization's success is *chosen* innocence. To him, there is a kind of innocence that is weak and helpless, like that of a very young child. At the same time, there is also the innocence on the "other side of wholeness"—a mature, loving, chosen innocence that is less self-conscious and driven by ego. Leaders who choose this innocence have a "purity of heart and intent, with a spine of steel."

The French philosopher Paul Ricoeur also has observed this chosen naivete/innocence. "Beyond rational and critical thinking, we need to be called again. This can lead to the discovery of a 'second naivete,' which is a return to the joy of our first naivete but now totally new, inclusive and mature thinking."

It's not just me, Chaudhary, and Ricoeur who aren't afraid to own being naive. Neither are some of these other impressive people:

*"This may sound a bit naive, but
I got here by believing in big dreams."*

—**HOWARD SCHULTZ, FORMER CEO OF STARBUCKS**

*"I was always . . . naive enough to not know
what I could not accomplish."*

—**KEVIN PLANK, FOUNDER OF UNDER ARMOUR**

"It is well for the heart to be naive and the mind not to be."

—**ANATOLE FRANCE, AUTHOR AND NOBEL PRIZE WINNER**

As mentioned in the introduction, this book will share short stories and business practices of others who have chosen to live a bit more naively. None are perfect, and like all beliefs, there is potential good and bad that comes with wherever you land on the spectrum. Rather than instructing you in something like the "seven characteristics great leaders need," this book is more reflective in nature and invites you to think critically about the ideas presented. In fact, we likely need to *unlearn* a lot more than we need to learn in order to embrace a *chosen* naivete.

In his book *Unlearn*, author Barry O'Reilly describes unlearning as a "process of letting go, reframing, and moving away from once-useful mindsets and acquired behaviors that were effective in the past, but now limit our success."

I agree mostly with this definition. But I also see it as a bit of a coming home—not just a "moving away from." You see, I believe you already have what you need deep inside of you, and you've had it there from the start. Something natural, authentic—*nativus*—naive. In these next chapters, make space to listen to it and help it grow.

To start, let me introduce you to Yvon.

Chapter 2

The Authentic, Unconventional, and Intentional Yvon Chouinard

Clunk clunk clunk clunk.

The '39 Chevy had just experienced its nineteenth flat tire. Finally fed up, the teens stuffed the back tires with grass and weeds and inched the last miles to Mazatlán. The surf was calling, and they weren't going to let this little hiccup ruin their school holiday plans. Or the fact that they couldn't afford medicine and were constantly getting sick from the bad water during these quick adventures down to Mexico. I mean, it's nothing that couldn't be treated with a classic cocktail of salt, water, and a little charcoal from the campfire, right?

From an early age, Yvon Chouinard knew his priority whether climbing, fishing, or surfing: *be outside.*

It likely comes as no surprise that Yvon wasn't too fond of school—except for the times when he could use it to further his true passions, like the moments in history class when he practiced holding his breath. Why? So that on weekends he could free-dive deeper to catch more seafood off the California coast. School and work just seemed to get in the way.

Climbing towering walls of granite in Yosemite became one of Yvon's greatest joys. It was from these experiences that he started to find an area of work he could enjoy. More out of necessity than anything, Yvon began to make some of his own climbing hardware.

Using a forge, anvil, and other tools, Yvon the self-taught blacksmith would make carabiners, pitons, and other gear for himself and his friends. While this started to bring in a little money, Yvon and his friends were still self-described rebels and took pride in the fact their climbing had no economic value in society. "Politicians and businessmen were 'greaseballs,' and corporations were the source of all evil."

While it was obvious Yvon had no desire to be in business, he found he could fuel his climbing passion through sales of more gear and a little scrappy living. For weeks at a time, he'd live on less than a dollar a day via an old army surplus sleeping bag and creative food choices, like buying cases of dented cat food cans from a damaged food outlet.

Eventually, demand from other climbers was so strong that Yvon put out a mail-order catalog to start advertising his climbing gear and had to hire a few climbing buddies to help with fulfilling orders. The year was 1965, and Chouinard Equipment was officially born.

From the beginning, quality was of utmost importance. They were making gear for themselves and their friends; if a piece of gear were to fail, it could kill someone. This focus on quality made it difficult to make a highly profitable business, but that wasn't the reason Yvon was doing it. Even still, by 1970, Chouinard Equipment was the largest supplier of climbing hardware in the United States. At the same time, it was slowly becoming an enemy to Mother Nature. To understand this, you have to know a few things about the era and the type of climbing Yvon and his friends loved doing.

Imagine staring up at a large, imposing wall of granite. Let's choose El Capitan in Yosemite. Standing a bit more than three thousand feet above the valley floor, it is roughly more than three times as high as the Eiffel Tower in Paris.

Most climbers will take several days to climb this majestic rock, finding spots throughout the ascent to rest and sleep by hanging hammocks or portaledges suspended hundreds or thousands of feet in the air on the face of the rock. Naturally, you would want to be 100 percent confident this hammock was going to hold you throughout the night.

In Yvon's early days, the way this was done was by pounding pitons—metal pegs—into the natural cracks of the rock face. These pitons and other securing devices were used—and hammered—throughout the ascent to also secure the ropes for the climber. Over many years, the repeated hammering of the hard steel pitons began to severely disfigure the rocks. Yvon saw this destruction firsthand at many of his favorite climbing spots. He was disgusted and had a big decision to make. What did he care more about: his growing business or the activity he loved and the environment that supported that activity?

Yvon and his team chose the latter. In their riskiest move to date, the 1972 mail-order catalog of Chouinard Equipment began with an editorial. "No longer can we assume the earth's resources are limitless; that there are ranges of unclimbed peaks extending endlessly beyond the horizon. Mountains are finite, and despite their massive appearance, they are fragile."

The catalog highlighted the environmental hazards of pitons—their core business—and announced they were stopping production. In place of pitons, Chouinard promoted the idea of clean climbing and the use of a different type of securing device, which at that time was not popular nor trusted in most of Europe or the United States.

Yet, the editorial argued, this new approach caused relatively no environmental harm. By primarily wedging various nuts (chocks) or hexes into existing cracks, they would preserve the sport for future generations.

The bet paid off.

Within a few months of the catalog's mailing, customers were ordering the new clean climbing devices faster than they could be made. Yvon chose to do good even over the potential demise of his business. His reluctance to be a "traditional" businessman wouldn't stop there, yet he would be tested many more times throughout the history of his company.

Now, some of you may have never heard of the name Yvon Chouinard or the company that was his namesake up to this point. By 1973, the company had been slowly expanding into the outdoor apparel business and decided to officially put those lines of products under a new brand. Patagonia was born.

PATAGONIA'S EARLY YEARS

Throughout the rest of the '70s and early '80s, Patagonia had a number of amazing successes and fabulous flops. Functional climbing clothes were a staple, and sometimes a piece or two would become an underground fashion trend. Rugby shirts that were useful for rough climbs became prized by kids at college. The inability to keep up with demand led to contracting with a garment factory in Hong Kong, which almost bankrupt Patagonia due to late shipments and terrible quality.

Still, sales continued to grow in other areas while lenders made credit hard to come by. And all the while, Yvon continued to struggle reconciling his reality with the voice of his inner rebel.

"I had always avoided thinking of myself as a businessman. I was a climber, a surfer, a kayaker, a skier, and a blacksmith. Now, we have a heavily leveraged company with employees with families of their own, all depending on our being successful. One day, it dawned on me that I was a businessman. If I had to be a businessman, though, I was going to do it on my own terms."

—YVON CHOUINARD

Yvon's terms meant things like:

- Letting people dress however they wanted
- Providing flextime to employees so they could surf when the waves were good or ski when the powder was fresh
- Paying people when they stayed home to care for a sick kid (table stakes now, but unheard of over forty years ago)
- No private offices, even for the executives
- One of the country's first on-site childcare centers

This unconventional approach to management, coupled with great product design and distribution decisions, led to year after year of record growth. By the late 1980s, it was evident the company was growing at a rate that would make Patagonia a billion-dollar company within the next ten years.

Were they growing too much? And what impacts were the growing business and the overall economy having on the environment? Each time Yvon went back to his favorite childhood summer spots, he saw fewer wild animals, caught smaller fish, and suffered from the increasing heat. The inner rebel's voice grew louder.

Patagonia got more involved in local environmental efforts, from providing office space for activists to making financial donations. In 1986, Patagonia committed to donate 10 percent of profits each year to good causes and later enhanced that commitment to be 1 percent of sales or 10 percent of pre-tax profit, whichever was greater. The company also began to improve internal operations, like becoming the first mail-order catalog to switch to recycled paper and develop clothing from recycled fabrics, all while continuing record sales. It seemed Yvon and his team were balancing good business and using business for good.

Until 1991.

After years of endless expansion, the economy hit a slump. Patagonia sales "only" grew 20 percent that year, less than half of the growth of the previous years and well short of the growth built into the hiring and inventory plans. Costs and production had to be cut, debts had to be paid, inventory had to be dumped, and in what was described as the single darkest day of the company's history, 20 percent of the workforce was laid off.

The culture was like family. In fact, it *was* comprised of a significant number of family and friends, so the loss of 120 employees cut especially deep. By Yvon's own admission, the company had exceeded its resources and limitations. They had become dependent on growth they could not sustain.

Yvon looked around. What Patagonia was going through was happening throughout the globe. In the early '90s, warning bells were already going off about the irreversible damage being done to forests, water systems, and the atmosphere. The global industrial economy was also becoming dependent on unsustainable growth. Yvon knew if he was going to stay in business, he needed to not just do business by his own terms—he needed to completely break the rules of business.

A RENEWED PURPOSE

The views were breathtaking. Yet, their hearts were heavy.

The top dozen leaders of Patagonia, still raw from the recent events earlier in 1991, were walking through the mountains of Argentina, in the real Patagonia. The reason they were there? To truly discern *why* they were in business and what kind of business they wanted Patagonia to be. What came from that excursion and meetings over the following months became the bedrock principles and philosophies that still exist today and have made Patagonia one of the most admired companies in the world. Drawing from early stories and the love these individuals expressed for their products, customers, and the environment, the following "reason for existence" was shared. This was the "why" they were in business:

All life on Earth is facing a critical time.

The root causes of this situation include basic values embedded in our economic system, primarily valuing expansion and short-term profit over things like quality, sustainability, environmental and human health, and successful communities.

The goal of Patagonia is to operate in such a manner as to be fully aware of those elements of the economic system and attempt to reorder the hierarchy of corporate values while producing products that enhance both human and environmental conditions.

Just like when Chouinard Equipment put its core piton business at risk by promoting the concept of clean climbing, Yvon and his team would not let traditional approaches to business get in the way of the good they wanted to do in the world. They would use Patagonia's products, their supply chain, their customer and vendor relationships—all the *ways* they do business—as a means to authentically live out their values and hopefully inspire other businesses to do the same.

They knew they would need to be profitable to be sustainable, but it was clear that the achievement of profit was not the top priority, and growth and expansion were values *not* basic to the company.

To this day, Patagonia has been a leader in redefining for-profit business and capitalism. Consider just a few of the contrarian ideas and actions of the company:

Do as much business with as few suppliers and contractors as possible. Some would say this is naive and creates the risk of becoming highly dependent on another company, but that's exactly what Patagonia wants since often it means the other company is also dependent on Patagonia. Ultimately, everyone's potential success is linked. What's good for them is good for Patagonia and vice versa.

Try to raise the standards of all workers, not just your employees. Patagonia's Fair Trade Certified program is in 10 countries and reaches 66,000 workers, providing funding for increased pay and benefits such as childcare centers or better health care. Usage of the funds are decided upon by a democratically elected group in each factory.

Don't build a new building unless absolutely necessary. When Patagonia does build a new one, like an early three-story office building in Ventura, California, it was made from 95 percent recycled material.

Make a product that never wears out. In fact, one time the company ran an ad in the *New York Times* on Black Friday encouraging customers to break away from disposable fashion and buy only what they need. The ad featured a Patagonia jacket and the headline, "Don't Buy This Jacket." It then explained the resources required for its manufacture and encouraged customers to repair and recycle via the Patagonia Common Threads Initiative, which enables customers to send worn items back to Patagonia for refurbishment and resale.

As Patagonia continues to redefine the rules of business, its goal of inspiring others to do the same has also had a ripple effect:

1% for the Planet: The original 1986 giveback idea spawned a worldwide movement and today, 1% for the Planet is a growing, global network of more than 3,419 businesses. This expanding community supports thousands of nonprofit partners in more than 64 countries.

> *"This is not philanthropy. This should be a cost of doing business. It's paying rent for our use of the planet."*
>
> **—YVON CHOUINARD**

Organic and Recycled Materials: In 1996, Patagonia transitioned to using only organic cotton. "I can't reform the entire conventional farming industry, but I can ensure that Patagonia buys only organic cotton, and I can persuade other companies to buy it." Companies like Adidas and Nike have been following suit and also making the switch.

Benefit Corporation/B Corp: Many organizations are going through this rigorous accreditation or even shifting their legal structure to align with evolving beliefs about capitalism. Patagonia became the first official Benefit Corporation in California and a leader in the overall B Corp movement. There are currently over 7,000 Certified B Corporations in more than 90 countries and over 150 industries.

Patagonia is not the largest company. Despite this, Patagonia does many things within its reach to improve conditions as a whole. While the company cannot accomplish its goals on its own, Patagonia does strive to improve conditions for the environment and its workers and inspire other companies that by doing good, they can also do good business.

P.S.

As I was writing this book in September 2022, Yvon sent another Ripple (or tidal wave) of Impact into the world with the announcement of his succession plan. The Chouinard family transferred their entire ownership of Patagonia—at the time valued at $3 billion—to a specially designed trust and nonprofit organization. This move will preserve the company's independence and ensure that future profits are used to combat climate change and protect undeveloped land.

"Hopefully this will influence a new form of capitalism that doesn't end up with a few rich people and a bunch of poor people," Mr. Chouinard, 83, said in an interview. "We are going to give away the maximum amount of money to people who are actively working on saving this planet."

Chapter 3

Ripples of Impact and the Power of Beliefs

As we saw in Yvon's story, a key inflection point required Yvon and his leadership team to pause and reflect on their actions. They relied on their core principles and beliefs to guide their choices around staying the course.

Chouinard Equipment was flourishing in the early 1970s, selling as many pitons as it could make. And yet the company chose to stop; in other words, it voluntarily shut down its largest, most profitable business unit. Why? Because Chouinard Equipment didn't like how it was impacting the environment. That decision would have seemed naive or too morally idealistic to many businesspeople at that time (and perhaps today, as well).

Fast-forward to the exceptional growth Patagonia would experience in becoming a billion-dollar company: At multiple points along the way, Yvon and his team chose to reflect on why they were doing what they were doing. They changed the trajectory they were on based on their core values. Oftentimes, this would restrain their business growth—again, an unheard of practice in traditional capitalism. What should've been a so-called kiss of death has been anything but for Patagonia.

Are Patagonia and Yvon Chouinard perfect? Nope, and that's not the point.

Instead, what can we learn from Patagonia's many examples of how choosing principles over profit leads to even greater growth? For one, taking the time to pause and reflect is a crucial step toward evolved decision-making. As famed psychologist Carl Jung warns us, "Until you make the unconscious conscious, it will direct your life and you will call it fate."

Too often, leaders do not stop and *intentionally* reflect on how their beliefs and actions are evolving as they do business. Without this intentionality, a leader can get carried away in a cycle of inauthentic actions or decisions that may not ultimately land them where they or their organization wants to be. Think about the executive who keeps chasing the next goal, believing that finally *this* achievement will be the one to make them happy or fulfilled or that gets the organization where it finally needs to be. It's like a treadmill they can't stop, a cycle of behaviors that becomes self-reinforcing.

For the sake of this book, we're going to focus in on those cycles of behavior in business that involve other people: employees, customers, communities, and the environment. These cycles can create positive or negative feedback loops, resulting in what some psychologists call a vicious circle or a virtuous circle. In other circles (pun intended), this feedback loop is called the Pygmalion effect or a self-fulfilling prophecy. They both operate more or less the same way but with very different results. Both cycles look something like this:

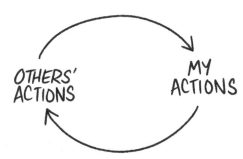

I help you, and then you help me, and then that makes me want to help you again—virtuous cycle.

I yell at you for cutting me off in traffic, you think I'm rude and speed up faster, and I get angry and slam the steering wheel—vicious cycle.

Yvon makes pitons so he can climb. His buddies want to buy them. Yvon makes more. His buddies and their friends buy more, etc. Vicious cycle or virtuous cycle? Depends on your perspective. From a utility perspective, it's a virtuous cycle. But from an environmental perspective, it's a vicious cycle. Taking the time to pause, reflect, and align with core principles led Yvon to prioritize environment over utility. And while it hurt his short-term profitability, it led the company to explode to levels of growth that would not have otherwise been possible.

Could Yvon have predicted this was the correct decision with enough rigor and rational analysis? Possibly. But the world is complex and uncertain. You need to bring more than just the logical side of an argument to the table. Yvon looked inward to understand what was genuine and authentic to what he truly believed, and he kept testing those beliefs.

Let's apply this to our model above. While still keeping this idea overly simplistic, we'll add in another element, inspired by Bob and Judith Wright of the Wright Foundation in Chicago:

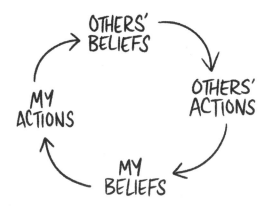

My actions don't always get a mirrored response from another person. Just because I help you, you don't automatically turn around and try to help me. Just because I make something and want you to buy it doesn't guarantee you'll actually buy it.

My actions go through a filter, which we'll simplistically call the "beliefs" of the person on the other side of the action. That filter has a way of shaping the interpretation of actions and the resulting reaction. Earlier today in an effort to be helpful, I asked one of my colleagues a few questions about a project he had been working on. He started off open to the questions, but after I asked a few more, he blurted out, "Don't you trust me to get this done on my own?"

Just because I believe I'm helpful—and then act in a helpful way—doesn't mean it will be interpreted that way. My act of "helping" might run into another person's belief that their boss doesn't value or trust them enough. They see my help, consciously or subconsciously, through a lens of mistrust and respond with a "no, thanks" or walk away. That action then comes back around and may influence my beliefs about being helpful the next time a similar situation comes around.

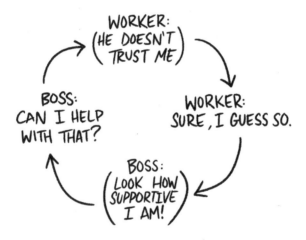

If you think that virtuous and vicious cycles can be complex, you're correct. Because of the filters of belief, it is possible for misinterpretations to create unintended and inaccurate vicious cycles. While this complexity is unavoidable, the solution is ubiquitous. When we pause and reflect, we can attempt to uncover the root of what's happening and address it directly.

The key to evolving our business practices to do more good in the world lies in the beliefs that impact those practices.

As each cycle comes back to the top, you have a choice. Dr. Fred Kofman calls this your "response-ability" and contends it is one of the most fundamental aspects of being human. You cannot change the cards you are dealt in life, but you can always own the agency and the freedom you have to pause and make a choice. How will you let others' actions impact your beliefs?

Now, your beliefs aren't only shaped by the responses you get when acting on them. You have deep-seated beliefs, ideals, and morals shaped by a variety of internal and external life experiences. It is important, though, to recognize the role others' actions have on your evolving beliefs. And I'll argue it's even more important to understand the role your beliefs and actions can have on others' evolving beliefs.

This is why it's critical to understand the power of the vicious or virtuous circle. You can choose to participate in a continued downward spiral of beliefs and actions. Let another angry driver ruin your afternoon, or in future days, think twice about being courteous in traffic. In the business setting, maybe you meet hostility or disrespect from a coworker by dishing back even more disrespect since "they deserve it." And yet disrespect breeds disrespect, and distrust breeds distrust. These are not what we'd choose when thinking clearly in our best frames of mind. It is extremely difficult to disrupt a vicious, downward cycle and set it on a better course. But it is undoubtedly worth it.

On the other hand, you can amplify existing virtuous circles. Think of the countless stories of people who continually pay it forward with spontaneous acts of great generosity. It takes a catalyst to start that virtuous circle. Might it be you next time?

This is what we mean when we talk about Ripples of Impact. As Mahatma Gandhi said, "If we could change ourselves, the tendencies in the world would also change. As a man changes his own nature, so does the attitude of the world change toward him."

In Yvon's eyes, he disrupted the vicious circle of his piton business and set it on a flywheel guided by sustainability and core values. Through the team's choices (and editorial), they espoused their beliefs about clean climbing, putting those beliefs into action by replacing that entire business line and charting an otherwise unattainable growth trajectory.

Organic cotton, workers' rights, 1 % for the Planet, giving away the *entire* company to endow decades' worth of further climate change philanthropy: so many Ripples of Impact sent out into the world. To be the change we want to see, it has to start with the behaviors and actions we practice. And those actions start with our beliefs.

As you may have noticed or will read in the next chapters, some beliefs about business and people are evolving. Often those "do more good" beliefs may come across as naive to others, yet we need more people to lean into that *chosen* naivete. How have your beliefs about people and business evolved over the past few years? How might an *intentional* reflection on your beliefs shift your actions or business practices in the future?

If we believe people are worthy of trust and inherently good, those ideas can kick off virtuous, self-fulfilling cycles that can ultimately lead to better workplaces and communities— spaces where human potential can be more fully unleashed to work on the world's biggest problems. Think of these as *your* Ripples of Impact. It all begins, though, with your courage to act on those beliefs.[1]

---

1 If you want a fabulous book about many of the concepts from this chapter, check out *A Lapsed Anarchist's Approach to the Power of Beliefs in Business* by Ari Weinzweig. He's the cofounder of Zingerman's Community of Businesses, highlighted in chapter 13.

Chapter 4

Evolving Your Beliefs: A Profound Yet Simple Approach

"Hello? Josh? Are you still there?" Evan said over the phone.

I was sitting at the desk in my office, MacBook propped up on a stack of books. As I blankly stared at the exposed brick wall beyond the computer screen, I shook my head a bit.

"Maybe. I'm not sure," I answered.

Evan laughed. As my executive coach, he was used to my poor attempts at humor.

Attempts at bad humor aside, what Evan had just shared hit me like a bolt of lightning, so my answer was an accurate description of what I was feeling. An insight of this enormity is best described as an epiphany.

Years later, I would thank Evan and ultimately point to that moment as a pivotal contributor to who I am today. To appreciate why it changed my life so much—and why it might change yours—let me provide a little more context.

Like most people, I grew up in a world that put an inordinate amount of focus on the idea of winning or losing. Sports, video games, school: it all seemed to thrive on the idea of rankings and competition. Later in life, I saw more of the same in the workplace, community organizations, and even in my family. I was constantly looking at decisions and trying to deduce how I stacked up, what a win was for my business, my family—even my life. Often, though, it felt like when I "won," *someone* or *something else* was losing. To use the words of the great philosopher Ricky Bobby, "If you ain't first, you're last."

But Ricky Bobby was wrong about this (and many other things). Eventually, I realized the highest ideal was to approach life in pursuit of the "win-win." Master negotiators are renowned for finding solutions that leave all parties happy. But it is also as simple as my wife picking dinner and me picking dessert. Finding a win-win solution was never easy to pull off, but when it worked, it seemed like nothing could possibly top it. In the world of win-lose, the win-win had won—until that call with Evan.

With decades of corporate experience and advanced training as an executive coach, Evan had become a trusted advisor for me. Besides referring him to friends and clients, I would occasionally hire Evan myself for some personal and professional coaching. The exchange I described at the beginning of the chapter was one of those times.

In preparation for that particular conversation, Evan had asked me to complete an assessment to examine how I take and give energy in my leadership approach. As he reviewed my results with me, I saw this table in the report:

7 LEVELS OF LEADERSHIP ENERGY

1 - VICTIM	"I LOSE"
2 - ANTAGONIST	"YOU LOSE"
3 - RATIONALIZER	"I WIN FIRST, AND THEN YOU CAN WIN"
4 - HELPER	"YOU WIN"
5 - COLLABORATOR	"WE ALL WIN OR NOBODY PLAYS"
6 - CREATOR	"WE ALL ALWAYS WIN"
7 - PASSION	"THERE ARE NO WINNERS OR LOSERS"

I stared at that bottom line, Level 7: "There are no winners or losers." The descriptor on the next page of the report went further: "Winning and losing are illusions."

There are times in your life when something just clicks. If I could rewind and watch my life, I'm sure I would have heard versions of this message in the past. For some reason in this moment, with this combination of words, my mind was ready to receive the message. It felt like an out-of-body experience as my mind rushed through dozens of memories where I had felt the joys of winning or pains of losing. Those times certainly did not feel like illusions when I experienced them. But it was suddenly clear to me: my perception of those things that were won or lost was exactly that—my perception.

Carl Jung once said, "The greatest and most important problems of life are all in a certain sense insoluble. They can never be solved, but only outgrown." My attempts to figure out how to "win" in work, family, and life always seemed to fall short. After earning that promotion I desperately desired or getting that new car I wanted, I always ended up envisioning something else. The happiness of those wins was quickly replaced with discontentment, discouragement, and even suffering as I set my sights on the next achievement or win.

Yet in this moment with Evan, I understood how I was creating my own suffering because of the lens through which I had chosen to view a particular situation. When presented with the idea of winning and losing as mere illusions, I realized this was what Jung was talking about. This was not a problem for me to solve; it was a problem for me to outgrow. From that day on, I considered the ideas of winning and losing more loosely, and the results have been transformative.

AN APPROACH TO EVOLVING BELIEFS

Beyond my epiphany, how was I able to make this change stick? Around this same time, I was introduced to a self-inquiry framework that helped me adapt to my evolving beliefs. Based roughly on author Byron Katie's work in identifying and dealing with stressful thoughts made popular in her work and books, including *Loving What Is*, the framework goes something like this:

Identify an existing belief.

Reflect on the following questions:

- Where did I learn this belief?
- Is this belief absolutely true?
- What do I gain by holding this belief?
- What do I lose by holding this belief?

Be open to shifts in perspective about this belief.

Here's a few observations about the questions, and then I'll provide an example.

First, it's important to clarify what a belief is. I like the way Kevin Bermingham says it in his book, *Change Your Limiting Beliefs*:

> Beliefs are simply a feeling of conviction or certainty that something is real or true. They're based on our past experiences and what others have taught us. Beliefs are our best guess at reality—our mental model of how the world appears to work. Our knowledge of the real world is limited. So to get by, we rely on our beliefs instead. They're the principles and rules by which we assume the world works.

Because beliefs are our best guesses at reality, we can't be 100 percent certain they are absolutely correct. There is always an element of faith when we're talking about beliefs. Being open to the idea that our thoughts and beliefs can evolve over time is a powerful concept. Decades ago, the futurist Alvin Toffler predicted things like the internet, genetic engineering, and rampant consumerism. He also popularized the notion that "the illiterate of the twenty-first century will not be those who cannot read and write but those who cannot learn, unlearn, and relearn."

With the rapid pace of change and increasing complexity in our world, you are not *required* to constantly evolve your beliefs, but the ability to pause and reconsider a previously held "truth" or belief is going to be more important than ever. Unlearning will be as important as learning. And given what we know from behavioral science, that is a hard ask. To have a shot at overcoming our own bias, we must make space and be intentional.

Second, I appreciate that the questions assert there is always something to be gained or lost by holding a particular belief.

Beliefs give us a mental model to navigate our lives. As the statistician George E. P. Box quipped, "All models are wrong, but some are useful." While he was describing specific scientific models and formulas, the idea still applies here. No mental model we have of the world can be 100 percent correct; our personal knowledge of the world is limited and constantly changing, not to mention colored by our own biases. Yet that doesn't mean the mental model or belief should be discarded.

We need models, principles, and beliefs as lenses to help us perceive reality and go through life. Why? In some studies, the processing capacity of the conscious mind has been estimated at 40 to 120 bits per second. Yet the amount of information coming at us continues to increase and is closer to 11,000,000 bits per second. That is way too much information for us to process, so we rely on these lenses, albeit imperfect ones, to help us survive and act in a semicoherent way.

APPLYING THE QUESTIONS

So let's put this framework to use. In the beginning of this chapter, I described a belief I held about winning and losing. Let's call it: "Always seek a win-win."

Where did I learn this belief that a win-win is always the right approach? While I don't recall the specifics, I'm pretty sure the idea of competition was cemented early on in sports and at school. I played soccer growing up, and the idea of "everybody gets a trophy" was not quite introduced yet. Winning and losing were quite evident on the soccer field. And in academics, it was pretty evident through grades, scholarships, and activities how achievement and winning were perceived and treated. Yet later in life, I saw specific business instances firsthand that created or worsened inequities in the workplace and found the wisdom in the adage, "A rising tide lifts all boats." My belief was established, and I sought more win-win solutions in life.

Is this belief absolutely true? I had assumed so up until that call with Evan. I had experienced some pushback to this belief in action, as I would receive critiques that my pursuit of a win-win solution or compromise sometimes left a lukewarm feeling in opposite parties on an issue.

What did I gain by holding this belief? I suppose I felt like I was getting the best of both worlds: a drive to win but a feeling of something greater by also focusing on how others could win. I gained admiration from some for being seen as a caring, considerate leader.

What did I lose by holding this belief? This is always a hard question to answer. If I'm honest, I definitely lost the respect of some people who didn't feel like I was driving hard enough for one particular win over another. I remember receiving a particularly painful 360-degree leadership evaluation that called this out. I also had this nagging suspicion that when I did achieve a win-win and some people were still "meh" about the compromised outcome, it meant people were still losing something.

No belief or model is perfect. This belief, though, had served me pretty well. I wasn't looking to consider something else. What I was losing by holding this belief wasn't painful enough for me to actively question it. But for some reason,

Evan's call cracked open something that had me consider a shift in belief. Let's call the evolved belief "Winning and losing are (sometimes helpful) illusions."

Now let's repeat the exercise.

Where did I learn this belief that winning and losing are an illusion? You could fill in this one for me. I learned it during that call with Evan. Upon further reflection, though, I think there were seeds of this idea planted earlier in life in the different facets of philosophy and religion I had come across.

Is this belief absolutely true? Maybe. The more and more I use this question, the more I like the fact that it is often a rhetorical question. Don't skip it; it's mental priming for the next two questions.

What do I gain by holding this belief? It is really hard to put this belief into practice. I can still get worked up about a perceived loss. Last week, we found out a client chose another consultant to work with instead of us. When I'm at my best, I can catch myself and really see that the story of loss I'm telling myself is just that—a story. We can still learn from that perceived loss and do better next time, but the emotion and suffering I used to feel are less connected to the situation. Sound like a Jedi mind trick? It's taken a lot of practice, and this reframing definitely doesn't happen often enough. I'm an imperfect person, and I especially fail at this when I'm tired, stressed, or hungry.

Another interesting point is that letting go of the need for a win-win has actually made it easier for me to accept that a win-lose situation is often required for some of the world's most complex problems when someone might lose in the short run. For instance, Pacha Soap Co. (highlighted in chapter 15) loses out on significant short-term profits and endures logistical headaches by choosing to take on underrepresented suppliers in third-world countries.

What do I lose by holding this belief? Yes, there are definitely things I lose by holding this belief. In a world dominated by winning and losing, some people think I don't take things seriously enough. And in some instances, they're right. I can come across as naive. I also confuse people sometimes because I do believe the *concepts* of winning/losing can be helpful for some to achieve what they need at their particular stage of life while still holding them as simple *concepts*. This paradox frustrates some people.

Now, I'm not asking you to believe what I believe. In fact, I intentionally chose one of my beliefs that is definitely not mainstream. As you can see, both in what I used to believe and what I believe now, there are things that work and things that don't. Like you, I have imperfect mental models, and old be-liefs served me quite well for most of my life.

I invite you to pause at this point and think of a belief you hold—any belief. It could be about the world, your business, or about yourself. Take a moment and see if you can track it back to the source. Who planted the initial seed of that belief? What has strengthened or reinforced it over time? How long have you held it? Do you know anyone who holds an opposing belief about the same subject? If you held that opposing belief in-stead, what sort of things might you be doing differently in life?

The point of this book is to share stories of successful lead-ers doing things a bit differently than others, maybe even you. Their mental models and beliefs are imperfect yet might get you to think about things a little differently. My invitation to you is to be open to other beliefs that some traditional busi-ness leaders—even you—might think are unworkable and be-gin to understand that what is or isn't naive is all a matter of perspective.

At some point in this book, a part of you may retort, "I want more evidence," or, "Where's the business case and empirical proof?" When you hear that voice, thank it. It has likely served you well for most of your life. Then apply the questions above. What do you gain and lose by holding the belief "I need more proof" before trying something new? Part of the aim of this book is to bring that rational part of you (and your business) into better balance with the other important parts of your mind: the intuitive, emotional, and spiritual.

The next section of the book consists of micro-chapters, each focused on short stories about a particular belief or evolving business practice. At the end of each chapter, you'll be invited to practice the questions above. I hope these stories inspire you to think a little differently and a bit bigger about how you create success and joy in your life and business.

Part 2

THE PRACTICE

Behind every managerial decision or
action are assumptions about human
nature and human behavior.

—Douglas McGregor,
The Human Side of Enterprise

Chapter 5

Unlocking Tools: How a Naive, Lazy Boss Liberated a Factory

Yesterday, my daughter broke her phone.

It was one of those slow-motion-worthy fumbles out of her postworkout, sweaty hands.

Crack. Screen down, right on the pavement: teenage life emergency. We had phone insurance through Asurion, and at 6:00 p.m., I was on the phone with a delightful agent named Jake. He promised a new phone would be express shipped to my home by noon the next day. And to our amazement, it was. Thanks, Jake.

Now reflect on that story for a moment and how far we've come as an industrial society. Imagine how it would sound to your great-great grandparents.

My teen daughter had a micro supercomputer in her hands. It broke, and a new one was shipped halfway across the continent in less than a day. Wow! And we have some people around my great-great grandparents' age to thank.

Huge strides were made during the process of industrialization that helped us get to where we are today: Frederick Taylor's insistence on dividing work among managers and workers; Frank and Lillian Gilbreth's motion study research that led to breaking down jobs into their microcomponent tasks; Henry Ford's popularization of the moving assembly line. All of these great advancements in the early 1900s turned manufacturing and its laborers into a well-oiled machine.

This led to significant output and efficiency gains on the factory floor, not to mention other industries. In many ways, this "well-oiled machine" approach also led to significant advancements for consumers in terms of affordability and availability of goods, higher profitability for shareholders, and to a more limited extent, better working conditions and take-home pay for the laborers themselves. At the core of this approach, though, are some beliefs about people and the most effective way to do business that are increasingly coming under more scrutiny.

For instance, here's a belief espoused by the father of so-called scientific management:

> *"The man who is physically able to handle pig-iron and is sufficiently phlegmatic and stupid to choose this for his occupation is rarely able to comprehend the science of handling pig-iron."*
>
> —**FREDERICK TAYLOR**

Beliefs like this one, and many others, were used to justify the current command-and-control practices many modern organizations are now trying to evolve away from.

So what does this evolution look like in practice?

THE NEW BOSS

Jean-François Zobrist had been on the job for only a few months as the new CEO of the FAVI manufacturing plant. Because of his recent arrival, he was trying to learn as much as he could and intentionally trying not to make any sudden changes.

One day, he was walking the factory floor when he came across a man named Alfred. Alfred was a machine operator, working in a part of the factory dedicated to automotive parts, but Jean-François did not find him in his corner of the factory. Instead, Alfred was patiently waiting in front of the storage room.

"What are you doing?" Jean-François inquired.

"I have to change my gloves. I have a coupon from my boss and my old gloves," Alfred said.

Jean-François was about to learn of a rule at FAVI. When an employee needed new gloves, he first had to show his old gloves to his boss to receive a coupon. With this coupon, the employee proceeded to the storage room. Once he arrived at the storage room, which was locked, he had to ring a bell and wait for the employee in charge of the storage room to come. The worker would then receive new gloves in exchange for the coupon and the old pair of gloves.

In Alfred's particular instance, Jean-François noted this took about ten minutes. Why did Alfred have to go through this process? Well, because they needed to keep their supplies and tools under lock and key in case a worker would steal them. Seems logical, right?

Curious, Jean-François went up to the accounting department and learned that the machine on which Alfred was working cost the company around $1.75 to operate every minute. FAVI couldn't just shut down the machine for the short time Alfred was away. If Alfred wasn't at the machine, the company would lose almost $2.00 a minute.

The new gloves only cost about $1.00 per pair. So in reality, spending ten minutes off the machine meant the gloves were costing almost eighteen times as much as what they had thought! In a later interview recalling this incident, Jean-François said, "It made me realize that this process was making the gloves a bit expensive. And that, without promoting stealing, even if [the gloves were not locked up and] the employee was taking a pair from time to time for gardening, everyone would largely win." This sparked some of the first changes Jean-François Zobrist decided to make as the new CEO of FAVI.

THE LIBERATION

Based in France, FAVI had been in business for twenty-five years prior to Jean-François's appointment as CEO. FAVI is a manufacturer and supplier of technical parts for a variety of industries, principally the automotive industry. When Jean-François arrived, the factory floor he inherited was largely indistinguishable from any other down the road. Workers clocked in and out to mark their shifts. Every minute late resulted in a deduction from their pay. All machines and operators were monitored for hourly performance. Every output below the hourly target also resulted in a dock in pay. All tools, consumables, and safety equipment were locked up for fear of theft.

Jean-François had already decided he wanted to "unlock the tools." As he started to propose additional changes to his senior management team, he met resistance. How would they be able to keep people in line if they started to relax some of the controls they had in place? Finally, Jean-François had enough and decided to make a bold set of changes all at once.

On the last working day of the year, just before the Christmas break, he assembled the entire workforce in a corner of the factory. Standing on top of a few boxes, he shared that the way people were controlled in the company felt disgraceful to him.

After the holidays, there would be no more time clocks. A fixed salary would replace the variable pay system—no more pay deductions to try to control people. The supply room would be unlocked, and everybody would be trusted to take out the supplies they needed and log what they took out for reordering purposes. Even the managers' canteen would be closed, and everyone would have lunch together.

In a final symbolic move, Jean-François had a brick wall built in front of the large glass observation window that managers used to look down on the factory floor—no more watching over the shoulders of workers from the ivory tower.

Jean-François recounted some of the inspiration he was feeling at the time in his memoir, *The Story of FAVI: The Company That Believes That Man Is Good.* "We were only demanding hands and muscles from our employees . . . I was dreaming of a place where everyone could use his brain and his heart. A place where employees are seen as reasonable people who can be trusted to do the right thing."

 He realized that the organization chart was still built on the assumption that humans are bad. Jean-François continues in his memoir, "Based on the works by McGregor and Maslow, I enjoyed designing a different organization chart built on the assumption that 'the human is considered good.' People always tend to act as they are considered. If we open the spaces of freedom, people will start developing themselves and they will set themselves ambitious targets."

Think back to the vicious and virtuous circles we discussed in chapter 3: Many early management controls were built on condescending, negative beliefs like the one shared at the start of the chapter. On the contrary, by believing and acting on the idea that people are good, you increase the likelihood that they will indeed act that way . . . and believe that about themselves. This proved to be the case at FAVI.

During the years after the company was "liberated," productivity increased significantly. Jean-François recounts, "At that time, we did lots of metal cutting work. In the factory there were around twenty hydraulic presses aligned, all operated by women. And the same women, on the same machines, were now producing 20 percent more pieces per shift. And I observed a second unexpected effect. Normally everyone arrived at 6:00 a.m. in the factory to wait in front of the time clock. Now, everyone arrived at 6:00 a.m. at their workplace and started their working day directly. The same happened in the evenings. Suddenly it became common to witness a worker stay another fifteen minutes to finish filling up their cart for that day. Normally workers would already finish their day of work and would be waiting in front of the time clock for several minutes."

At FAVI, the average production time of its main products went down from eleven days to only one day! For more than twenty-five years, the company achieved over 20 percent annual net cash flow and eventually gained a 50 percent market share in the European automotive industry in its niche. Employee turnover was lower than the industry average, and the quality of product continued to increase, while prices did not.

Many people believe giving freedom and trust to workers in a factory or production setting is naive. Jean-François would actually agree. In fact, his second book is called (in English) *The Company Liberated by the Naive and Lazy Little Boss*. Can you imagine what the organization would be like if Jean-François hadn't chosen to be a little naive? FAVI would say that if loving the customer and trusting in mankind is naive, so be it. The results show what can happen if an organization truly attempts to unleash the full potential of its employees.

So what do you think? Is it foolish to put so much trust in workers, to unlock the tools and do away with time cards? How much control are you willing to give up as a leader in order to give that control to the employees? What do your practices today say about your beliefs in other humans?

DARE TO BE NAIVE

Let's apply the reflection questions.

Choose a belief statement below that resonates
fully or partially with you or come up with your own
around a topic in this chapter. This is about exploring
perspectives, not about convincing you one way is
right over another.

The vast majority of people can be trusted to not steal.

*People need accountability and controls in order to
perform their best.*

*Docking pay for tardiness and lack of productivity
are effective forms of management.*

At their core, every person is good.

(Something else you come up with!)

Got a belief statement? Good. Now, reflect on the
story as well as your well-earned life experience
and answer the questions to the right.

Where did I learn this belief?

_____
_____
_____
_____

Is this belief absolutely true?

_____
_____
_____
_____

What do I gain or would I gain by holding this belief?

_____
_____
_____
_____

What do I lose or would I lose by holding this belief?

_____
_____
_____
_____

Chapter 6

Inspired Engineering: Designing Love into Algorithms and AI

The subject of the email was intriguing.

A new job we think you'll love!

Teri double-clicked on it and read the first line of the message.

"While we know you're currently working in quality control, there's an open position in the finance department that seems to match some of your interests. Care to learn more?"

Teri had never considered working in finance. After further review of the job opening, she was amazed at how much she resonated with the opportunity. She decided to submit her interest in the role and set up an interview with the hiring manager.

Over one thousand miles away, Manisha Singh was likely smiling. Last spring, as she recounted this situation during our interview, it was clear she was a different type of leader—

one who would always question the status quo, even if others thought her naive. As the principal architect behind the new internal talent mobility platform at this Global 500 company, she was proud of the artificial intelligence (AI) they had built into the system and the results it was having for people like Teri.

Not surprisingly, the journey to launch the system was full of much fewer smiles, but not for the reasons you'd imagine. Sure, there were the typical technology and implementation migraines you expect from introducing a new platform to 140,000 employees in over 100 countries. The unexpected hand-wringing came from an unlikely source: how much *love* to design into the open talent market concept and AI.

A few years earlier, the easiest way for employees at Schneider Electric to find another job within the company was to go to the company's external LinkedIn page. Then, they would find a posting they were interested in and apply to the hiring manager. Definitely not the best employee experience, yet typical for many global companies. Manisha proposed the idea for an "open talent marketplace" and worked with her team to develop a solution. This was a disruptive and pioneering concept in 2017, and Manisha was one of the few in the corporate world who dared to bring it to life.

Manisha and team conceptualized a single marketplace for empowered people to choose jobs, projects, and coaches at any point in their career—without needing permission from anyone.

She partnered with HR leaders and explored the policy changes needed to enable something as audacious as this. Together, they worked on designing the concept, educating the business, and gaining critical alignment to pilot this novelty. Finally, they began the design phase for the platform itself.

Countless vendors were considered and eventually rejected because their approach to solving the problem didn't match up to the ideals Manisha and her team were interested in living out through the new system. These ideals, or design principles, would eventually lead even Manisha's own team to deeper reflection on their beliefs. What did they believe to be true about people? How would this new system reflect that?

For starters, how involved would human resources be in this new talent marketplace idea? Would they allow people to directly apply for jobs without being recommended or vetted by an HR business partner? Should an individual's boss have a say in whether or not they get to apply for another job within the company? Who should be copied on emails at what stage of the process? Whose needs were ultimately most important here, the employee's or the organization's? Could we trust the technology? Could we fully trust our employees?

The answers to these questions were exponentially important because they influenced the design principles for the concept and became embedded in the workflows. These beliefs would influence the algorithm used by the AI. That ripple would be felt throughout the system thousands of times a day.

Their eventual solution? Train the system to prioritize an employee's preferences *even over* the organization's preferences.

Manisha's beliefs on these matters were pretty clear: "My personal mission in life and at work is to design a future that loves us all. We have the power to shape our future rather than be passive recipients of what unfolds. My deliberate inclusion of 'love' speaks of a world with a place for all, with diverse individuals, organizations, communities, and societies."

How did that translate to this project? The team designed into the system many beliefs that prioritized active concern for the care and growth of the employees, including:

> *Equity is important.* Just because you sit closer to the manager doesn't mean you are the best person for the job. People far removed should also have equal consideration.

Autonomy and freedom are preferred. A person's manager may not always know what's best for them. Running the process through these managers adds to bureaucracy.

People have the ability to reinvent themselves. Manisha believes we have the infinite ability to become who we want to be at work, just like we keep growing into multiple roles in our personal lives. If someone expresses interest in an area outside of their current expertise (like Teri), that should be honored and they should be encouraged to explore that.

It's important to be ethical and trustworthy. AI datasets and algorithms have to be explainable to employees and must be used for scalable implementation. Yet there should be a human in the loop for making final choices. Additionally, the power of search should be included to counter the echo chamber effect of recommendation engines.

While it took a lot of skillful diplomacy, dialogue, and deliberate communication to convince HR and operational leaders to choose this path, the open talent market platform ended up being a huge success. Employee engagement, productivity, new skills development, internal efficiencies, and filled jobs all were benefits of this intentional approach to designing from people-centered beliefs. Many other multinational companies have since taken the approach that Manisha and her team co-created with this vendor. "I feel proud to have pioneered the concept of open talent marketplaces and helped make the world of work a little better than what I found."

Admittedly, this intentional approach to people-centered design and transformation has been a struggle at times for Manisha—not due to her own convictions but in how it has been received by leaders in business across the globe.

She has experienced too many transformation projects that look good on paper but never end up changing things—projects that put the key performance indicators ahead of people and never end up actually moving the needle on those KPIs. In those situations, Manisha advocates for putting people first even when it requires an investment of time and a steely resolve on her part. Having over twenty years of experience in global leadership roles, she knows it is ultimately better for business in the long run, but many leaders still push back on anything that sounds too "naive."

> If you care for people, if you truly love them, then they will really work for you. You don't have to micromanage them or create random benefits which sound exotic but do not make a difference in meaningful work or experiences. You don't have to use a carrot and stick model of rewards and motivation. People will go above and beyond. They'll surprise you.

And if leaders still don't believe Manisha, well, in those moments, she remembers they are rejecting the idea, not her.

> If I'm on the right path and I'm still facing 90 percent rejection, it's only because they are not able to see it yet and I haven't found the right way to show them. I'm really motivated by the possible upside of doing something in a disruptive way, in a more human way, and with empathy. If we do this right, we create a precedent for everyone to follow, like with the open talent marketplace.

Fortunately, Manisha has observed many such successes in her career that give her hope. Early in her career, these successes and stories helped plant a seed about the infinite potential inside each human being.

PEOPLE-FIRST AT TATA GROUP

From the early days of manufacturing locomotives to the recent years of Jaguars, Land Rovers, and other vehicles, the Tata Group has always needed more engineers. As Manisha's first job out of university, she relished the people practices she observed while serving as an HR business partner to some of Tata's largest factories in Pune, India.

One practice in particular caught her attention: the graduate Engineer Trainee Programme. Factory line workers who wanted to pursue the path of engineering could apply to the program and go through the same assessment and hiring panels as those coming out of the university with engineering training. With a focus on developing the raw potential of any worker willing to put in the effort, countless individuals were able to step into this program and increase their opportunities in work and life. This program yielded many successful leaders across various fields: manufacturing, R & D, employee relations, and even HR. Manisha fondly remembers how one of these leaders became her role model and mentor as she landed as a new recruit in Tata Motors.

This care for employees should come as no surprise from an organization that has routinely been commended for its HR practices. The roots of love for employees go back to the earliest days of Jamsetji Tata when he started Central India Spinning, Weaving and Manufacturing Company in the late 1800s. In his plants, he installed the first fire sprinklers and humidifiers in all of India. He began a pension fund paying accident compensation and started an apprenticeship program—developing that innate potential within each person. Contrast that with other workplaces at the time where compensation for injury—even death—while on the job was practically nonexistent. These and many other people-centered decisions were decades ahead of the competition at that time.

Over one hundred years later, Manisha learned some of these same values and continued to practice them at Tata and beyond. On one occasion later at Schneider Electric, she had the opportunity to hire seven individuals for a digital transformation effort. After evaluating all the candidates, she made seven offers, and over half of them surprised her peers in HR and IT; four of her new hires had no relevant IT experience. Manisha was again starting from the belief that people have the potential within them. With the right vision, coaching, and mentoring, the entire team, including those four, was very successful on the project.

Today, Manisha is an executive partner in the talent transformation practice of IBM. She is passionate about the future of work and how, through intentional design, the infinite potential within every individual can be unleashed. The Ripple of Impact from that "unleashing" will help us realize the potential of our organizations and wider societies to do more good.

"Even if I fail, even if I don't succeed, it is worth the try because if I do . . . it has disproportionate value on the impact it can create for others."

—MANISHA SINGH

So what do you think? Is it naive to believe you can design love into the systems at work? What about starting from the assumption that all people have innate potential?

DARE TO BE NAIVE

Let's apply the reflection questions.

As you read some of Manisha's stories, what did you feel? Let's take one of those ideas through our reflection questions. Remember, this is about exploring perspectives and helping you to think bigger.

All people have innate raw potential.

Love does not have a place in the work environment.

Systems should be designed to help employees grow.

Managers know what is best for their employees.

(Something else you come up with!)

Got a belief statement? Good. Now, reflect on the story as well as your well-earned life experience and answer the questions.

Where did I learn this belief?

_____

_____

_____

_____

Is this belief absolutely true?

_____

_____

_____

_____

What do I gain or would I gain by holding this belief?

_____

_____

_____

_____

What do I lose or would I lose by holding this belief?

_____

_____

_____

_____

Chapter 7

Giving More: A Hotelier's Approach to Karmic Capitalism

Did you know the impact some charities have is one hundred or even one thousand times as much as others when given the same amount of resources?

My friend Colin had just shared this fact with me, and I was curious. One of the core values in our company is "Give More," and hearing that there was a way to give more *effectively* was intriguing. Colin was introducing us to some of the core ideas in the effective altruism movement, and we decided to dig in more.

As an example, if you have a concern about animal welfare, there is a bit of an imbalance in where advocacy dollars are directed. Nearly ten billion animals live and die in factory farms in the United States every year, many in spaces where they can't even move or are subjected to cruelties, like castration without anesthetics. Ouch.

> *"Effective altruism is about asking 'How can I make the biggest difference I can?' and using evidence and careful reasoning to try to find an answer. It takes a scientific approach to doing good."*
>
> —WILLIAM MACASKILL

About seven million animals pass through pet shelters each year in the United States. This is 1,400 times *fewer* animals than go through factory farms, yet pet shelters receive donations of about $5 billion annually, compared with only $97 million given to advocacy groups trying to improve factory farming. If you think of the marginal utility of one more dollar to either of these causes, giving to those focused on factory farming has a high possibility of being more effective.

Admittedly, thinking more intentionally about the ripple effects of how I spend my time or money for good was a hard but helpful exercise. It required introspection personally on *why* my own family gives and *how* we make those oftentimes less than thoughtful decisions. I didn't completely overhaul our family's approach to giving, but I did shift some ways we give. For example, the next time a colleague sent us a request to help with their American Cancer Society fundraiser, I sent half of the money we normally donate. I then sent the other half to the Against Malaria Foundation, a top-rated charity based on GiveWell's research criteria for effective charities.

Of course I wanted to support my friend who was raising money in honor of someone who had cancer. At the same time, I'd learned that the American Cancer Society is extremely well funded and therefore, dollar for dollar, I can have a greater impact on the world by helping fight malaria in a developing country. Pausing to stop and reflect on the beliefs that inform our practices is hard and helpful work. Seeing how those beliefs evolve into new practices over time, even in business, can create opportunities for doing more good.

What might it look like if you committed to a consistent practice of reflecting on your beliefs?

THE JOY OF LIFE

"From the outside, it seemed as though I was very successful, but it felt as though I had sold out."

Selling commercial real estate during his undergraduate years, Chip Conley admits he was still trying to figure life out. After receiving his MBA, he continued semisuccessful attempts in real estate until he finally placed his first bet in the hotel business. With his father as a lead investor, Chip bought the Caravan Lodge: "a bad hotel in a bad neighborhood [the Tenderloin, San Francisco] that nobody wanted." As his mother recounted to the magazine of their alma mater, "He took a really stupid step." Then she corrects herself. "He took a really gutsy step. He had no business going into the hotel business at all. It never occurred to me that he would ever make something as big as he has. It blows my mind."

Eventually, Chip would be credited with helping create the boutique hotel category. Started in 1987, he ultimately grew Joie de Vivre Hospitality to fifty-two properties. After Joie de Vivre's successful acquisition, he joined the leadership team at Airbnb as the head of global hospitality and strategy. His role as a mentor and "modern elder" to the three cofounders of Airbnb inspired a later book called *Wisdom at Work: The Making of a Modern Elder* and his current primary project, the Modern Elder Academy (more on that later).

Through all of this, Chip showed a knack for constantly reflecting on his beliefs and evolving the way he approached life and business. His approach to business was characteristic of someone who thrived on disrupting the status quo—for good. During his early years at Joie de Vivre, he was constantly refining ways to give more.

> *"I'll never forget the look on the face of one of our new Joie de Vivre general managers when we told him that one of the metrics that would define his performance was how much money he spent in serving discounted or free nonprofit groups in our hotel."*
>
> —CHIP CONLEY

At the time, this and other experiments Chip was trying might have seemed naive to traditional hospitality leaders and investors. But Chip was playing a much longer game, one coming from a deep belief in reciprocity and putting into the world what you would hope to receive yourself. A journalist in 2001 coined the term "karmic capitalism," and the phrase stuck.

I first met Chip in 2008 and got to observe Joie de Vivre Hospitality up close. It was obvious Chip was ahead of his time in understanding the virtuous cycle (chapter 3) that happens when you build an excellent culture that leads to enthusiastic staff, which generates amazing customer loyalty and ultimately, profitable business results. Yet there is an authenticity in the approach that Chip described to me:

> When you're in a place where you can invest love and care into people in such a way that they truly feel met as opposed to feeling like a cog in the wheel . . . People know there's a genuineness to it. It is coming from a place of humanity and from a place of joy and affection. All of that, to me, has been the way that helps create an enterprise that feels like love is woven into it without using the word.

This is extremely admirable, and I think the idea of karmic capitalism goes a bit deeper.

What does karmic capitalism look like in practice? Well, when Chip received a call from Liz Lambert, an individual looking to start a boutique hotel down in Austin, he volunteered to send the general manager of his flagship hotel, The Phoenix, down to help her for a few weeks. There was no immediate gain to be had from this, and it really came out of Chip's love for her passion and joy in her work. "I wanted her to succeed. I didn't know how or if it would ever pay me back in life."

Personally, Chip has selflessly made time on many occasions for idea sharing, questions about life, and cheering on my projects, like this book.

RIPPLES OF IMPACT

If you recall, before starting Joie de Vivre, Chip had a number of experiences in commercial real estate and other traditional business paths. These really turned him off to the idea of business overall. When he eventually did start his own company, he began a regular practice of self-reflection that has helped him further refine and shift his practices and beliefs over time. Even to this day, ten years after successfully exiting Joie de Vivre, he continues evolving:

> As a for-profit entrepreneur, I spent the first half of my life focused on return on investment (ROI). Now, I'm spending the second half of my life focused on a different form of ROI: Ripples of Impact.[1] When you drop a pebble in a pond, it creates a series of ripples that cascade out over the water. In our relationships, our emotions can create positive or negative ripples. The same is true in our businesses. The choices we make on where we purchase, how we build our company culture, and how we affect our community make a profound difference—sending energy into the world that will create positive or negative ripples.

---

1 And to give due credit, the catchy "Ripples of Impact" phrase came from Chip's colleagues, Justin Michael Williams and Shelly Tygielski.

Chip's latest projects are equally as inspiring. The Modern Elder Academy, a school and experience that helps reframe the midlife crisis into a calling, opened in southern Baja in 2018. MEA Regenerative Communities, a revolutionary approach to building an intergenerational, residential community, will launch in New Mexico in 2023. The goal for both of these endeavors? Designing space for people to evolve. To me, this is just a continuation of something that Chip has been doing most of his life through business: finding ways to give more. It represents a potential higher calling for all of us to aspire to in the work settings we create.

So what do you think? Is it naive to give more, especially in business?

DARE TO BE NAIVE

Let's apply the reflection questions.

Let's take it through our reflection questions. As always, choose a belief statement below that resonates fully or partially with you or come up with your own around this topic.

What we do in business can have Ripples of Impact, positively or negatively.

Make as much as you can now, and then later you can give back. Don't mix the two.

What goes around comes around.

It is important to build in reflection time and evolve how we give.

(Something else you come up with!)

Got a belief statement? Good. Now, reflect on the story as well as your well-earned life experience and answer the questions.

Where did I learn this belief?

_____

_____

_____

_____

Is this belief absolutely true?

_____

_____

_____

_____

What do I gain or would I gain by holding this belief?

_____

_____

_____

_____

What do I lose or would I lose by holding this belief?

_____

_____

_____

_____

Chapter 8

Side Hustles: Encouraging Work beyond the Job

Craig Moody heard a knock on the conference room door and looked up to see one of his employees with a concerned look on her face.

"Craig, I didn't sleep well last night," she started. "I did three TV interviews yesterday for this community advocacy work, and I'm starting to feel guilty about how much time it's taking away from my actual job."

Craig looked at one of the most senior members of his team and thought for a moment. Finally, he responded, "Grace, does it fuel your fire?"

She teared up a bit. "Absolutely, Craig, absolutely."

Craig encouraged Grace to keep doing that community work, and they continued on with their workday. As a managing principal and cofounder of Verdis Group, Craig Moody sees it as his mission to create space that catalyzes positive systemic change. And that absolutely includes space for his team members to grow, even if he can't draw a direct line between those efforts "outside of a person's actual job" and the next client project his team could work on. For Craig, though, it goes even one step further. "I'm interested in helping you make a better version of you. That could mean you aren't with our company in five years, and that's okay. We want to be an accelerant for whatever your growth path is."

Letting people work on side projects or even have side hustles may seem naive to some, but for this rapidly growing sustainability planning and implementation company, it's a way of life. Verdis Group collaborates on climate action and sustainability initiatives for complex organizations, which include cities like Omaha, Nebraska, or Salem, Oregon; institutions like the Seattle Aquarium and expansive public school districts; and large companies. In its core work, Verdis Group helps organizations see the multiple stakeholders they serve.

For instance, the aquarium isn't just serving the people passing through the turnstiles. Its stakeholders include government officials, conservationists, foundations, philanthropists, employees, corporations, and even the marine animals themselves. This wide, multi-stakeholder view of its work easily translates into the work environment Verdis creates for its employees. Each person working at Verdis is a whole person with multiple stakeholders and demands in their lives that go far beyond the expectations of their "actual jobs." And they are members of a much broader ecosystem that goes well beyond the walls of Verdis Group both in time and space.

Considering all of this, it becomes easier to see how Craig's management approach makes sense. If he were only interested in the outcomes of Grace's work on her "actual job" and the short-term outcomes of Verdis Group, then anything outside of that might seem like a distraction. But Craig holds the outcomes of Verdis Group a little looser and thinks through the implications of being one part of a multi-stakeholder ecosystem.

> *"We're going to trust karma that we're sending people out in the world to do cool stuff. If they're having a great time, if they're learning, if they're enjoying themselves and meeting people, things tend to work out."*
>
> —CRAIG MOODY

BACK AT HOME

My team has run things at Econic in a similar fashion. We've explicitly stated that people have permission to work on a side hustle and we'd love to hear about it. One team member has continued to pursue a special coaching certification, and occasionally, he'll pick up side gigs directly with clients. It's up to his discretion if he wants to run that work through Econic or not. I've had others challenge me and, of course, call out this practice as naive. "People will just take advantage of you and keep collecting a paycheck yet spend too much time on things that don't benefit the company."

In our experience, this hasn't been the case, and everyone reciprocates the trust extended to them. Furthermore, if there is a question about the amount of pay someone is getting as compared to what they are giving back to the company, that is a different issue that can be solved in a different way altogether. That is more a conversation around expectations and performance systems.

I hear the "people will take advantage of you" comment most when people talk about salaried individuals. There is fuzziness around how much time the company "deserves" based on the pay an individual is receiving. Again, this is more an issue with performance systems and comes from an increasingly outdated idea that companies are merely "renting" a person's time.

Switching to an approach that focuses more on the outcomes a person produces versus the number of hours they put into something leads to greater engagement and results. This became even more apparent during the recent pandemic as it became harder for managers to physically see people's time in office chairs.

Verdis and Econic are not alone in encouraging side projects or side hustles. The training firm Rebel Business School actually includes a clause in the employment contract giving consent to the idea. Tribal Worldwide London, a 150-person digital agency, has employees running Etsy shops or starting subscription businesses on the side. Even the CEO at Tribal has run a record label on the side for the past twenty years. These leaders cite that having outside interests helps diversify the team and actually creates more interesting conversations with clients. And more often than not, your employees are already doing these side projects. Your openness to talking about them just brings them into the light.

Encouraging employees to take their focus off their "actual job" can seem counterintuitive. That said, Ben Whitter, an HR expert and author of the book *Human Experience at Work*, said business progress is now more closely aligned "with the wants and needs of human beings." Side hustles and projects can be an important part of this because they allow people to take even more ownership of their growth and development, as well as design the lives they want to live.

"People are more interested in experiencing joy and freedom rather than being stuck chasing promotions and unnecessary status symbols," says Whitter in his book. "Make no mistake, employers are on notice. If they can't support people to live their best life, then employees will continue to take matters into their own hands. The costs associated with this will be too much to bear for many organizations."

So what do you think? Is it naive to let employees have side hustles? What about well-meaning projects outside of traditional work hours? In the new "always on, work from anywhere" sort of world, how much does the line begin to blur between what is "company time" versus "your time"?

DARE TO BE NAIVE

Let's apply the reflection questions.

Let's take it through our reflection questions. Challenge yourself on this one and maybe even try a belief you disagree with.

We can encourage side projects or side hustles.

If people have time for a side hustle, they aren't working hard enough.

We can help accelerate a person's growth, regardless of whether they are with us in five years or not.

What people do outside of work hours is up to them.

(Something else you come up with!)

Got a belief statement? Good. Now, reflect on the stories and answer the questions.

Where did I learn this belief?

_____

_____

_____

_____

Is this belief absolutely true?

_____

_____

_____

_____

What do I gain or would I gain by holding this belief?

_____

_____

_____

_____

What do I lose or would I lose by holding this belief?

_____

_____

_____

_____

Chapter 9

Deploying Conscious Capital: A Remix of Business and Leadership Jazz

"Business books are boring," Olivia replied.

My friend, Tim, had just asked his college-bound daughter to read an early draft of the first chapter of this book. To further make her point, she added, "The only way I'd work at a business is if they try to do more than just make money."

Now, Tim's daughter is a pretty conscientious person. After spending a few days touring college campuses, Tim shared that she noticed the beautiful facilities and events but wasn't swayed by them. "Olivia was more impressed by the focus on sustainability, philanthropic opportunities, and programs aimed at helping students, such as UC Santa Barbara's free food market [for people in need]."

It's apparent to me that Olivia and her peers expect more from business. At the start of this book, I referenced a study based on the United Nations Sustainable Development Goals (SDGs). These goals are focused on global imperatives, like ending poverty, providing clean water and sanitation, encouraging responsible consumption and production, creating sustainable cities, ensuring quality education, and twelve others. In a recent international survey, 81 percent of millennials believe businesses have a key role to play in achieving the SDGs. In an even greater demonstration of the values reordering, 75 percent of millennials said they would take a pay cut to work for a socially responsible company.

With this in mind, companies must demonstrate a commitment to sustainability if they want to stay relevant to younger generations of customers and employees. Luckily, we have some leaders who have been working for the last couple of decades to help businesses do more than "just make money."

EARLY DAYS OF CONSCIOUS CAPITALISM

"*How* you make the money is as important as how much money you make."

This is just one of several nuggets of wisdom Jeff Cherry shared on a recent podcast episode of *Capitalism: The Remix*. On each episode, Jeff interviews diverse entrepreneurs and thought leaders on topics that will ultimately help listeners create more value for their businesses and their communities. When it comes to running businesses that care about *how* the money is made, Jeff is full of wisdom, and he should be; he's been working in the field known as conscious capitalism for decades.

Conscious capitalists focus on using business to elevate humanity, moving to the idea of results and accountability around people, planet, *and* profits. While a for-profit company needs profit to be sustainable in the long term, how you treat people and the planet is ultimately accretive or dilutive of your financial bottom line.

In 2013, Jeff started the Conscious Venture Lab to help incubate and invest in new start-up companies with this stakeholder capitalism approach baked into its DNA from the start. He helps manage the Conscious Venture Fund, which aims to invest in companies out of the Lab and other for-profit organizations aligned with the mission. This is extremely important because a lot of capital available to companies comes from investors who believe the *only* way to maximize a return on their investment is to pit shareholders against, as Jeff says, "all of the other stakeholders a company must engage in order to create *real* value."

Those investors might see extra costs related to sourcing more ethical ingredients or providing unique well-being benefits to employees as superfluous and taking away from the maximization of profit. Several years prior to these two ventures, Jeff was already working with other alternative investment management companies focused on sustainable businesses—back before the book *Conscious Capitalism* had even been written. Jeff is on a mission to provide alternate, values-aligned funding sources to these companies as well as spread the news and facts that doing good in business is actually *good for business.*

"I call this the 'paradox of purpose,' and I've seen it play out more times than not," Jeff shared.

"When organizations start to pay as much attention to how they make money—how they treat their employees, how they treat the environment, how they serve the customer—it almost always leads to making more money."

—**JEFF CHERRY**

It was clear from Jeff that the focus has to be on the means and that the means are connected to your purpose. The moment that the leader is doing all of those "nice, naive" things only because it will make them more money, people sniff that out. It isn't authentic.

While Jeff has seen this paradox at play in the companies he's helped launch in the Lab or invested in through their funds, his very first experience in thinking about *how* the business was done came during his initial career in architectural design. Jeff was faced with figuring out how to coordinate the people around him at a firm he started just a few years out of college. "I had just come out of school to be an architect; they didn't teach us much about management or things you'd learn in a traditional business school."

The year was 1986, and the first thing he had to tackle was setting up the organization. To him, the old model of a top-down, command-and-control pyramid structure just didn't feel right. "And maybe it was my own lack of confidence in not feeling like I had earned the right yet to tell people what do to." Either way, Jeff was interested in a more collaborative, people-centered approach to setting up the business and coordinating work. He found inspiration in several places, including a discussion he once had with ex-CEO of Porsche

Peter Schutz, emphasizing a more democratic, consensus-based approach to leadership.

> I was also inspired by the book *Leadership Jazz* by Max De Pree. Like jazz music, the leader in the organization has the responsibility to set up the structure, but everyone gets to play their instrument. The leader isn't telling you how to play your saxophone or what to do when it's your solo. The band knows the general tune they're playing, who the audience is, and the mood they're trying to create. As long as they sort of play within those boundaries, things are great.

As Jeff applied this approach to his design firm, people were happier and felt more freedom to be who they really were. It helped him see that the purpose of business wasn't just about making money but also about how you made people feel and treating people the way you would want to be treated. This revelation really struck home for Jeff and has been a defining part of why he cares so much about evolving the way business is done. "Growing up, and even to this day, I see friends and family members who seem to only be working for the weekend. It makes me viscerally sad to see how draining their work is to them and how they are rushing through most of their week to get it over with."

Jeff's friends and family members aren't the only ones. Year after year, Gallup continues to report 60 to 80 percent of workers are disengaged or actively disengaged. Work does not have to be this way and can actually be a vehicle for human flourishing when leaders begin to care about *how* they make money as much as how much money they make.

And what would the world look like if businesses and investors cared about how money was made *even more* than how much money was made? I bet Jeff's paradox of purpose would play out even in that naive dreamworld too.

DARE TO BE NAIVE

Let's apply the reflection questions.

It's reflection question time! Choose a belief statement and really challenge yourself to think about what you would gain and lose by holding this belief.

Work can be a vehicle for human flourishing.

If you're working with public capital and investors, how much you return is the only thing that matters.

How money is made is even more important than how much money is made.

You can't take care of people if you don't make a profit.

Taking care of people, customers, and the environment can actually lead to making more money.

(Something else you come up with!)

Got a belief statement? Good. Now, reflect on Jeff's stories as well as your well-earned life experience and answer the questions.

Where did I learn this belief?

_____

_____

_____

_____

Is this belief absolutely true?

_____

_____

_____

_____

What do I gain or would I gain by holding this belief?

_____

_____

_____

_____

What do I lose or would I lose by holding this belief?

_____

_____

_____

_____

Chapter 10

Sharing Ideas: Loosening the Grip on IP and Trade Secrets

Want to know Coca-Cola's secret recipe?

How about Colonel Sanders's closely guarded eleven herbs and spices?

Two all-beef patties, *special sauce*, lettuce, cheese, pickles, and onions on a sesame seed bun?

For many restaurants and food companies, landing on a successful recipe can be a gold mine. Many times, the secret will be locked in a vault, shared with only a few chosen people. Speculation and copycat recipes abound, but much goes into the protection of this "competitive advantage." This includes patents, lawyers, isolated (and more costly) manufacturing, and supply chain approaches to keep the secret safe. So when you run into the exact opposite, it can be a bit jarring.

LETTING THE SECRET OUT

I needed more salt.

My fingers looked like prunes, like I had been sitting in a bathtub for far too long, though it had been weeks since I'd taken a bath. I asked my wife what she thought.

"I don't know, maybe you're dehydrated."

If this was last year, we might have been a bit more alarmed, but this time, neither of us got too worked up about it. We both had gotten used to strange things happening with my body, as it had been months since I started a new healing program to rid my body and gut of a massive gastrointestinal bacterial overgrowth, a yeast infection, and a sneaky, immunosuppressive parasite that we affectionally named Pendejo.

It was a trifecta, as my doctor had called it a few months back. "With that luck, you should probably go bet on the horses," she joked as she initially reviewed my lab work and prescribed several medications and dozens of supplements to begin healing and rebalancing my body. I had experienced many peculiar side effects as my body began to heal, but this prune finger thing was new.

I reached out to my doctor, and she confirmed that I likely was dehydrated. At the time, I was eating very few processed foods to not irritate my gut as it was healing, and I likely was not getting enough sodium. The doctor recommended adding a daily electrolyte supplement, which would make it the fifty-second pill/spray/drop/mix I was putting into my body daily. Granted, I was only on this healing regimen for (pruney fingers crossed) a couple months longer, but it still felt like a ridiculous amount of things to be taking and an equally ridiculous amount of money to be spending monthly on the program.

Before this experience, I had never been a vitamin or supplement person. Who knows, maybe that's one of the reasons I ended up with my "trifecta"? It always felt like most vitamin or supplement companies were trying too hard, marketing too much to get my attention. It made me suspicious. If you have to convince me that much that I need your product, I skeptically thought, I must not really need it. That's significant, coming from the guy writing a book on naivete.

Most advertisements felt like they came with shaky promises and were based on shakier business models. Now to be fair, I was noticing drastic changes in how I was feeling during this journey to heal my gut, and I did credit a lot of the supplements and prescriptions I was taking for that shift. Having lab work to back up the doctor's recommendations aided my belief in the first round of things I was putting in my body. And I could definitely see my pruney fingers were coming from something. So when my doctor suggested that I needed to add an electrolyte supplement, I started to research the one she suggested.

The mix she recommended was called LMNT and was marketed as an "all-natural, zero-sugar, paleo-keto friendly, hydration mix." What a mouthful.

After reading reviews on their website and others, I clicked on the "shop" tab at the top of the page and decided to purchase a twelve pack to try it out. As I was about to click over to the purchase page on mobile, I noticed a FAQ section. I kept scrolling.

The very first listing in the FAQs was titled "Homebrew Guide" and said: "Want to make your own electrolyte drink mix at home with LMNT ratios?" then proceeded to give the instructions, ingredients, exact measurements, etc., to make your own version of LMNT at home.

I sat back in the couch, stunned.

This was unlike my impression of other vitamin and supplement companies. By providing their specific recipe, weren't they undermining their business? Couldn't competitors just copy them? Or couldn't people like me just close out of the purchase screen and go make it themselves? (Spoiler alert: the primary ingredient was table salt, which was sitting less than thirty feet away from me on the kitchen table.)

Curious about why this company would be so transparent with their intellectual property, I spoke to LMNT's CEO, James Murphy.

"Our company is rooted in supporting people on their health journey. If they use LMNT, great. We most care about health outcomes, and there are many paths to get there," James shared. He also reiterated that the recipe isn't rocket science, so pretending like it was wasn't authentic. "The simple fact is: Most folks need more salt. Period. Just plain and simple NaCl. And an early draft of our website said on the homepage, 'It's just f*cking salt.' So truly, there is no secret."

We live now in an era where food sources and transparency are more valued than ever. Sharing the exact recipe doesn't lessen my belief in LMNT as an expert or make me less inclined to buy their product. Instead, it strengthened my loyalty to their brand and made me trust its business a bit more. To this day, this supplement is still a regular part of my health routine.

LMNT's sharing felt authentic, like the company truly cared about *why* it was doing this. James even told me LMNT has found four other companies who have copied its recipe and to a certain extent, their branding and packaging. James's reaction?

"It's fine. It's like a friendship. Someone else having friends doesn't take away from my friendships and community. These markets are so big, and it's more generative, dynamic, and even fun to operate from abundance rather than pretending it's a zero-sum game."

SHARING MORE THAN JUST SALT

In 2012, McDonald's was asked by a customer what was in the Big Mac's secret sauce. Not only did they share the recipe, but McDonald's Executive Chef Dan Coudreaut did a YouTube video showing how to make it with ingredients you could buy at any grocery store. Other large companies followed suit, and over the years there has been a big rush of "secret recipe" sharing, especially during the recent pandemic.

Disney published a recipe for its famous churro bites. DoubleTree by Hilton and Pret a Manger shared their chocolate chip cookie recipes. The owner of the Bend Soup Company, Dave Johns, decided to share one of his secret recipes each week, saying, "It's more important to give people comfort during this time than to protect my soup recipes." And the fast-food mashup success of Taco Bell's Doritos Locos Tacos was developed over years without a contract and famously done on a handshake deal between the two company CEOs.

The trend of loosening the grip on intellectual property isn't just stopping with food. Elon Musk put out very detailed technical and business information on his Hyperloop transportation idea in a fifty-eight-page white paper and invited others to tackle building the technology. And 84 percent of the Fortune 500 use GitHub, the world's largest development platform that has a specific emphasis on open-sourced code and sharing.

As we've seen, it's traditionally been common business practice to guard information as closely as possible. For many, these secret recipes or ideas were seen as their competitive advantage. This may still be the case for the business you're in, and it may still have good justification, but more and more companies are rethinking this approach.

As information gets shared and copied faster and faster, the advantage goes to companies who have great cultures and can execute on an idea more so than those who merely come up with the idea. LMNT has many copycat competitors and yet has grown from $1.5 million to $50 million in annual revenue in just three years, and the growth isn't slowing down. As bestselling author and speaker Patrick Lencioni has identified in his research, "The seminal difference between the most successful companies and those that are mediocre has less to do with smarts and know-how but rather team-work and organizational health." With that shift in mindset, how might sharing what was once unshareable be to your advantage?

So what do you think? Is it naive to share the secret recipe or a proprietary idea? When would it make sense to hold some things back? When might it make sense to hold things a little looser?

DARE TO BE NAIVE

Let's apply the reflection questions.

———————————

Let's take it through our reflection questions. You know the drill.

The more people who know our secret recipe, the better.

We must guard our proprietary idea at all cost.

Execution on an idea is more important than the idea itself, so I don't care who knows the idea.

In our industry, intellectual property is king.

(Something else you come up with!)

Got a belief statement? Good. Now, reflect on the stories and answer the questions.

Where did I learn this belief?

_____

_____

_____

_____

Is this belief absolutely true?

_____

_____

_____

_____

What do I gain or would I gain by holding this belief?

_____

_____

_____

_____

What do I lose or would I lose by holding this belief?

_____

_____

_____

_____

Chapter 11

Unconventional Purpose: Using For-Profit As a Means to a Different End

Herb Kelleher, the founder of Southwest Airlines, coined the phrase "the business of business is people." It was a play on the quote by the late economist Milton Friedman who said, "The business of business is business."

Now, Friedman was a very well-respected professor and statistician. He even received the Nobel Prize in Economics. His argument in 1970 was that the only social responsibility a business had was to maximize its profits and shareholder returns. At that point, Friedman would concede, the investors could do all the charity work they wanted. You saw this play out many times during the 1900s, with famous examples like Carnegie, Rockefeller, Vanderbilt, and others amassing as much as they possibly could and then attempting to transform society through philanthropy, endowments, and grand visions.

A lot of progress was made through this approach. Unfortunately, though, a lot of harm and destruction also came from this sole laser focus on shareholder return. Issues around child labor, low wages, and no safety net for workers injured on the job were prevalent. Plus, many of the issues we're currently facing around climate change could in some ways be connected back to this tunnel-visioned approach to business. What scenario do you envision and feeling do you get when you read the phrase, "Sorry, buddy, it ain't personal. It's just business?"

At Southwest Airlines, Kelleher had a different idea about what business could and should mean. "The business of business is people." The first time I read it, I realized immediately why it resonated so deeply with me.

THE PEOPLE BUSINESS

In 2004, I started working for a training and consulting company with an audacious vision: "What would the world be like if everybody did what they were good at and enjoyed?"

We helped companies like The Ritz-Carlton Hotel Company, Mercedes-Benz, and Estée Lauder identify people's talents and fit them into jobs that aligned amazingly with those behaviors that came most naturally to them. Figure out what people love to do, see if your company needs that, and then match those things. Seems pretty simple, right?

Most of these organizations approached hiring in this way because it made good business sense and led to better customer service, among many other outcomes. One particular company, though, stuck out to me as unique among this list of elite organizations. Their unofficial motto? "We grow people through frying chicken."

Harman Management Corporation is not a household name, but the product and brand it launched is: Kentucky Fried Chicken. The story of how Pete Harman met Colonel Sanders in 1952 and began serving his signature chicken has been documented in a number of ways. Less known, however, is the eventual management philosophy that pervaded what at one time was the original and largest franchisee of KFC. Pete and Arline Harman, and their eventual HR leader Jackie Trujillo, claimed they were first in the people business, not the restaurant business.

Now, a lot of organizations claim they are "people-first" or "employee-centric," but at the end of the day, for many companies, these are shallow promises or simply words on a wall. What inspired me about the Harman story was this notion that the purpose of their business was much deeper than just serving food. It wouldn't have mattered if they worked in food service, manufacturing, agriculture, etc; they worked first and foremost for and on the development of people.

This permeated their culture and the systems developed as the organization scaled. For instance, they did not intend to create a system that made it likely for people to choose a lifelong career as an entry-level cashier. Harman did not want people to get comfortable in that job and halt their personal growth. They provided generous tuition reimbursement benefits. They provided robust management training programs, and it was their intention that people who started in that entry-level role either moved up into management in rapid succession or moved on to find another job or career. And if an individual wasn't on track to move into their management program, Harman helped that person find another job or take another step on their growth journey as they were exiting the organization.

To put the growth of people at the core of a for-profit business's reason for existence seemed astounding to me. And yet, the more I looked, the more I began to find other examples of businesses set up in this way. Here are just a few, highlighted in even more depth in great books like *The Healing Organization* by Raj Sisodia and Michael Gelb:

H-E-B is a privately held grocery retailer based in Texas, with more than one hundred thousand employees or "Partners," as they are known within the company. They're fond of saying, "We're in the people business, but we just happen to sell groceries," and it shows. H-E-B has given over one billion pounds of products to food banks and led disaster relief efforts rivaling the Red Cross and FEMA. The CEO has gone on record saying, "Pay our people as much as you can, not as little as you can. The income gap between top and bottom earners is too great for the nation's future stability."

You've likely never heard of Greyston Bakery, but you may have had one of their most famous products, a brownie so good it makes its way into every celebrated pint of Ben & Jerry's chocolate fudge brownie ice cream. Its business model is what should really be celebrated, though.

Bernie Glassman didn't start out with a dream to make brownies but rather went in search of a business idea he could use as a centerpiece to address the homelessness and poverty he was seeing in his community. The bakery created a low-skills-necessary environment where it could train anyone, especially those deserving a second chance in life, like the formerly incarcerated. Around the bakery, Greyston built housing, childcare, and health-care solutions to serve families. Consistently profitable and impacting thousands of lives each year, Greyston Bakery's motto is: "We don't hire people to bake brownies; we bake brownies to hire people."

The story of Bob Chapman and Barry-Wehmiller Companies is told remarkably in the book *Everybody Matters*. They have acquired more than one hundred companies, typically low-tech manufacturing businesses in small towns, with a focus on using these businesses as a source of enrichment and healing to the employees and those communities. Through "courageous patience" and love, leaders help instill a culture of continuous improvement and legacy building—both personally and professionally. The company has countless stories of how this approach has shifted the generational trajectory of families and their children.

When a business starts to believe and act in a way where "it isn't just business, it *is* personal," profound changes can happen. Decisions are made differently. Alternative measures of success are considered. Lives are changed—for the better.

So what do you think? Is it naive to think the core purpose for business could be about the growth of people? Is this easier to do when you're starting a business, like Greyston Bakery? Or might it be possible to apply to an existing business or even a team you're a part of, like at Barry-Wehmiller Companies?

DARE TO BE NAIVE

Let's apply the reflection questions.

_____

Let's take it through our reflection questions.
As always, choose a belief statement below that
resonates fully or partially with you or come up with
your own around this topic. Remember, this is about
exploring perspectives, not about convincing you
one way is right over another.

*The growth of the people in our company is more
important than most any other thing.*

*Putting people as the core business reason makes
it hard to do some things, like layoffs.*

*Having the development of people as your core
purpose and not a specific business model is freeing.*

*A business that only exists to hire and grow people
is bad business.*

(Something else you come up with!)

Got a belief statement? Good. Now, reflect on the
stories as well as your well-earned life experience
and answer the questions.

Where did I learn this belief?

Is this belief absolutely true?

What do I gain or would I gain by holding this belief?

What do I lose or would I lose by holding this belief?

Chapter 12

Trust Transactions: Lessons from Pay-What-You-Want Businesses

"Ok, but can't you do *any* better on this price for me?"

Standing at the jewelry counter, this seemed like a fair question. As a college student, I wasn't exactly rolling in money. At the same time, I was choosing to take on one of the most expensive single purchases I had made to date: an engagement ring.

My girlfriend, Trisha, and I had been dating for a few years by that time, and I had made at least a few jewelry purchases for her along that journey. Each time, regardless of the specific jewelry store, it felt like a can't-win guessing game to know what the actual price was going to be versus the price printed on the sticker or advertised in the display case. Sometimes it felt like I could get a huge discount; other times it seemed like the price barely budged.

Later in life, making my first car purchases, I found that this jewelry store negotiation game was mere child's play. I dreaded the final mile of a car purchase with all the secret message shuttling to the "manager in the back office" or the countless attempts to upsell after-market care or packages.

Now, some people do thrive in these types of negotiations, my dad being one of them. We used to joke that he would negotiate the price of toilet paper at Walmart if someone would listen. As for me and most people I know, arriving at the negotiated price of something felt uncomfortable at best, divisive at worst.

In recent years, several organizations, including car dealerships, have implemented greater pricing transparency and no-hassle purchasing. Some of the most intriguing experiments being run are in the space of "Pay what you want." Rather than being divisive, these purchases put the final cost partially or fully in the hands of the purchaser.

PRICE TRANSPARENCY AND BEYOND

Econic, our consulting company, was reviewing ideas to increase the transparency of our pricing to our client partners. A friend sent me an example of another consulting company she admired. As I clicked on the link she sent me, I saw a specific page on its website dedicated to rates. My heart raced as I scrolled through the description of its approach. The first thing that caught my attention was the company offered three different tiers of rates:

A **solidarity** rate of $75–175 per hour per trainer

A **full cost** rate of $175–275 per hour per trainer

A **redistribution** rate of $275–400+ per hour per trainer

The organization, AORTA, specifically calls out that it has a wide sliding scale of prices. "It is an intentional effort to distribute resources equitably between organizations we work with, including universities, nonprofits, cooperatives, and grassroots community organizations."

AORTA invites and acknowledges that those corporations that can pay at the higher end of that scale are indeed "redistributing" some of those funds and making it possible for AORTA to work with grassroots organizations at little to no cost to them. Most companies make enough margin to be able to give money back to charity or provide pro bono services. Until this one, I hadn't seen an organization be so transparent with the give back and show its largest, most well-funded client partners how they were supporting that giving.

As I scrolled further down the web page, a second thing caught my eye. The organization transparently breaks down how it uses the money it makes. For a sample daylong training, the web page shows what percentage of the overall price goes to salaries, benefits, independent contractors, and operating expenses. I could see how providing this level of transparency, as well as inviting organizations into helping them serve other smaller organizations, would build trust and a sense of community or communal good with their clients.

Pay what you want isn't just an experiment in the professional services space. In fact, it's more common in the consumer marketplace. The most successful applications of it utilize approaches that mirror some of what AORTA was doing: providing transparency and inviting the payer to consider how they are supporting a larger communal need.

The online retailer Everlane utilizes a limited choose-what-you-pay approach with its mostly discounted items. Shoppers for some items encounter three different prices. Hovering over the lowest price says something like, "$0 to Everlane: This only covers our cost of production and shipping." The middle price shows a dollar amount, variable based upon the actual price, and the message, "This helps cover production, shipping, and overhead for our seventy-person team." The highest price shows a larger dollar amount "going to Everlane" and messages, "This helps cover production, shipping, and our team and allows us to invest in growth. Thanks!"

Which option would you pick?

FURTHER RESEARCH

In a study conducted in Germany, researchers found that patrons at a deli and a coffee shop on average paid more to the store owner when presented with a pay-what-you-want option. They also felt it was a fair exchange of value and were more satisfied with the transaction.

In that same study, though, they saw that patrons paid considerably less to a cinema when presented with the same option. Some of the discrepancy? The analysis showed that the connection the patrons had to the food shop owner and the communal values she represented drove some of the difference.

This mirrors what another restaurant, Der Wiener Deewan in Vienna, has known and practiced for over fifteen years. This all-you-can-eat Pakistani restaurant has been successfully running off of a pay-as-you-wish concept since its inception. As the owner Natalie Deewan says, "We give trust, and it comes back! We can trust in people's capacity to think for themselves; if they did not pay at least a fair price and we therefore had to close, where would they find such a good meal for such a cheap price? Our customers are our community."

The restaurant chain Panera attempted a pay-what-you-can approach for almost ten years via their Panera Cares Community Cafes. Opening several locations during the 2010s, the nonprofit restaurants tried to redistribute services by nudging middle-class consumers to pay a little extra for their meals so that the cafe could provide free or reduced meals for those in poverty. Many of the critiques of the approach and why it was not ultimately a sustained success focused on poor design choices, brand confusion, and execution issues, not as much on the failure of the concept itself. On a smaller scale, cafes like this have worked and are still open, like Karma Kitchen in California and SAME Café in Denver, the latter being the initial inspiration for the Panera Cares concept.

So what do you think? Should we offer customers the opportunity to pay what they want? Is it too confusing to pull off or are there too many selfish people in the world to make it work? Or with a certain level of trust, community-mindedness, and authenticity, can it enhance business and its impact on society?

DARE TO BE NAIVE

Let's apply the reflection questions.

———————————————

Let's take it through our reflection questions.
As always, choose a belief statement below that
resonates fully or partially with you or come up
with your own around this topic.

*If you let people pay what they want, you'll often
be taken advantage of.*

*If you give trust, it will come back—even when
it comes to pricing.*

Transparency in pricing and costs can be a benefit.

(Something else you come up with!)

Got a belief statement? Good. Now, reflect on the
stories as well as your well-earned life experience
and answer the questions.

Where did I learn this belief?

_____

_____

_____

_____

Is this belief absolutely true?

_____

_____

_____

_____

What do I gain or would I gain by holding this belief?

_____

_____

_____

_____

What do I lose or would I lose by holding this belief?

_____

_____

_____

_____

Chapter 13

Being Intentional: Challenging Growth for Growth's Sake

"You're either green and growing or brown and dying."

A few of the other executives in the room nodded. I pushed a little further: "Is that really true?"

The tension continued to mount in the nicely appointed, modern-looking boardroom of this nationally known engineering firm. I was thankful two walls of the room were made almost entirely of glass. First, the bank of exterior windows let in a lot of sunlight and seemed to brighten the overall dim situation. Second, the glass wall separating the room and the well-trafficked lobby made it possible for any passerby to see what was going on in the room. Nobody was going to completely lose their cool if they knew others could see them. I empathetically pushed a little more.

"Your team should be very proud of the last twelve years of continued growth. All I'm asking you to consider is: Will it ever be enough? I have little doubt you'll hit one billion in revenue in ten years at the current pace. The deeper question I want you to reflect upon is: Why? Why are you growing?"

This can seem like one of the most ludicrous, naive questions you can ask someone in business. Do you want to grow your business? And if so, why?

There are myriad reasons why you would want to grow your business, and most of them make logical sense. For starters, publicly traded companies or those who take on outside capital generally have a mandate to grow or at least maximize the return to their shareholders. This often includes growth in traditional measures (revenue, profit, scale, etc.). A decline or stagnation in sales, market share, and earnings typically causes panic in these investors and then the company gets caught in a vicious cycle (remember those from chapter 3?).

Other times, a successful company is pressured into growth by *competitors* (we have to grow to fend them off); *suppliers* (if you grow, we grow); *customers* (you're so great, don't deny us your services and products!); or *family/friends/peers* (bigger is better, says society and my ego).

Frequently, though, leaders of companies do not stop and consider the alternative: they might be better off restraining growth. At the very least, stopping to be intentional and consider the *why* of growth is extremely important.

BACK IN THE BOARDROOM

The executive team took the prodding as I had hoped.

"As we keep getting larger, it takes more and more energy to convince our employees that growth is good for them individually."

The conversation switched to why they were in business. Stories were shared about the communities they've been able to serve, the projects that have created professional and personal growth for employees, and the large sums of money they were able to give to charity. At the heart of it, they recounted that they exist first and foremost for their employees. Any traditional growth that would get in the way of that motivation should be questioned. Growth for growth's sake wouldn't be tolerated. And yes, they even had a conversation about what the ceiling on their size could be.

Currently, this engineering firm employs about two thousand people and is between the third and fourth generation of being employee owned. The firm is motivated to provide a good financial return to these owners, and it is obviously a for-profit business. But this company, and progressively more companies, are recognizing they can challenge the prevailing assumption that you "just have to grow."

Recall those moments in Yvon's story in chapter 2. He knew Patagonia would need to be profitable to be sustainable, but it was clear the achievement of profit was not its top priority. As Yvon wrote, "Growth and expansion were values *not* basic to our company." At times, they even throttled growth because it conflicted with their core goals and beliefs.

Author and journalist Bo Burlingham coined companies like this "small giants." In his well-researched book of the same name, Burlingham shares the stories and lessons of companies who "were willing to forgo revenue or geographic growth, if necessary, in order to achieve other remarkable ends." If they did grow, it was more about opening up new possibilities for employees and the business. Growth was (sometimes) just a natural byproduct of the company's success in pursuing its real purpose. Here are just a couple highlights:

Zingerman's Community of Businesses in Ann Arbor, Michigan. After building a nationally recognized delicatessen with sandwiches "so big, you need two hands to hold," the founders were constantly being bombarded with ideas about franchising their business or opening new locations. Not only were there outside pressures, but internally, employees with great potential wanted new challenges. For two years, the founders wrestled with this idea of growth and ultimately landed on a different approach.

They would create a constellation of small businesses in Ann Arbor, each with its own unique offering and identity. All, though, would be designed to enhance the offering to Zingerman's customers and improve the performance of the overall company. They now have a bakery, a deli, a Korean restaurant, a candy shop, a training company, event and catering companies, a farm, a mail-order business, and several more. The Zingerman's Community is frequently benchmarked for its amazing service, approach to open-book management and finances, diversity, and sustainability.

Union Square Hospitality Group. Much has been written about Danny Meyer's inspiring approach to service and great culinary experiences. With twenty-eight James Beard awards, frequent #1 Zagat awards in New York City, and the successful launch and spin out of Shake Shack, there is much to be admired about USHG. In terms of the approach to growth, Danny originally deflected every shot at rapidly growing his award-winning restaurants. He even instilled a five-minute rule during the early years: no restaurant or project he was a part of should be more than a five-minute walk from his home in Union Square. This forced him to focus on what he most deeply cared about, which was the food and service experience—the soul of his restaurants.

Slowly and intentionally, the group tested out new restaurant concepts to provide platforms for employee growth. In the last decade, Meyer has shifted his take on growth, but the rejection of growth for growth's sake has persisted: "I now see that sensible, well-paced growth is essential to advance your culture. Because culture needs to grow. The worst thing you can do is try and maintain culture."

In his book, *How the Mighty Fall*, Jim Collins talks about the stage some successful companies get into called the "undisciplined pursuit of more": "Big does not equal great, and great does not equal big." Instead of getting preoccupied with revenue and size as a determinant of growth, the focus for excellent companies is the "right growth." Although complacency and resistance to change remain dangers to any successful enterprise, many of the mighty companies Collins highlights in the book succumb eventually to *overreaching*.

TOO MANY HANDS ON THE WHEEL

Aric was in the unenviable position of starting his business, again.

He and a partner had just repurchased the brand and intellectual property of XPLANE, the design consultancy that Aric had helped grow for more than a decade. That was before the "disease of growth" drove them to sell the company to a larger investment group.

"We grew eight years at a 40 percent compounded annual growth rate. In a people-intensive business, our capital requirements were outstripping our profits, and we couldn't keep up." Each new investor Aric and his partners brought into the firm increased the pressure to grow, which increased the need for Aric to find more outside capital. A vicious cycle, he later recalled in our interview. "I had one hand on the steering wheel, and it was being pulled by several other hands."

Eventually, that need for outside capital led to the acquisition by a larger company who was pulling together a handful of agencies, like XPLANE, in a roll-up strategy. Six months after the acquisition, though, the parent company decided it didn't want to be in the professional services business, and Aric was left with the unfortunate task of laying off most of his previous employees. This led to the eventual repurchase of remnants of the old company. As they restarted XPLANE, Aric shared that they took a long, hard look at their "why" of business. Rather than chasing a *growth* path like before, they spoke deeply about the pursuit of an *impact* path. Today, eight years after restarting XPLANE, Aric and his team are thriving in their efforts to "accelerate positive change through the people inside of organizations."

If you desire to chart your own course as a leader or business owner, being intentional about how and if you grow is paramount. If not, you'll be a servant to the customers, investors, suppliers, competitors, and society, who will make those growth choices for you if you let them. There will always be a business larger than yours, or more impact to make, or another market opportunity just out of reach. Take control and be intentional about *why* you're in business and *why* you would or would not want to keep growing your business, department, or practice area. Is it naive to think you have another choice to consider than just "keep growing"?

DARE TO BE NAIVE

Let's apply the reflection questions.

———————————————

Alright, let's take this idea through our reflection questions. Which belief below will you reflect on? What might be gained or lost by shifting to a new belief?

It's possible to have a successful business even if it isn't consistently growing.

You're either green and growing or brown and dying.

There are other goals more important than growing sales and market share.

Bigger is better in business.

Saying no to traditional business growth is scary.

(Something else you come up with!)

Got a belief statement? Excellent. Now, reflect and answer the questions.

Where did I learn this belief?

_____

_____

_____

_____

Is this belief absolutely true?

_____

_____

_____

_____

What do I gain or would I gain by holding this belief?

_____

_____

_____

_____

What do I lose or would I lose by holding this belief?

_____

_____

_____

_____

Chapter 14

People First: Prioritizing Employee Growth Even over the Company's

"Can you believe the effort she put into that?" I said.

"I know. We've got a big decision to make," Brian replied.

My cofounder, Brian, and I had just witnessed some magic. We had asked a potential new hire to put together a short design-thinking-focused workshop for us as a demonstration of her skills. She had interactive exercises, putty for me to fidget with, and sticky notes galore. We were amazed. And we knew our clients would be too.

You see, the small consulting company Brian and I had started eighteen months prior was at a milestone. We were ready to hire our first full-time consultant. By this time, we had a couple other employees and consistent contractors helping design and deliver innovation and culture projects for our clients. But this next hire was going to be a leap forward for us:

a senior consultant, coming on as a full-time employee and at a guaranteed salary that was more than either my cofounder or I were paying ourselves at the time.

We eventually fell in love with that workshop wizard, Nicole, and offered her the position. She joined our team and made an immense difference to our culture and work product as our small company continued to grow.

And then she left—after only eight months.

We were in a bind, yet I couldn't have been happier for her.

From my work helping companies with leadership and cultural transformation over the last two decades, I know it is common for managers to receive "the call." A great employee says they need to talk to you, the manager. "Let's grab coffee or schedule a lunch . . . I've got something important to tell you."

During that awkward meeting, they let you know they love the work but accepted a job with another company. It wasn't you; it's nothing personal; and it was a job they couldn't refuse. Transition plans begin, and the employee is on their way, and you, the manager, are either left a little shocked, relieved, or affirmed because you saw the writing on the wall.

In the last fifteen years, I've led several teams and had dozens of direct reports. As far as I can recall, I haven't had "that call." Even during these last couple years of the Great

Resignation and Reshuffle, the "we need to talk" email hasn't shown up. Now, that doesn't mean people haven't left my teams to pursue other jobs within the organization or even with other companies. We just always worked that out *together*. Nicole was not an exception.

Several months into working with us, Nicole shared with me that she had been contacted by a former leader who moved to Spotify (a dream organization) to start a new team in London (a dream location). She asked my thoughts on taking the interview, and our conversation centered around how this opportunity could align with some of her dreams and goals. She did the interview, and a few weeks passed until I heard the next update. Nicole and her husband had been invited to go visit some of the Spotify locations in Europe to interview with potential team members.

We figured out how to cover work while Nicole took the trip and explored what this might mean for her and her family. Halfway through the trip, Nicole called me from London, and we discussed the pending job offer—not as a negotiation *against* what she was currently doing at Econic, but as a coaching call thinking even further about how she should approach the job they were offering her, the salary requirements, moving costs, etc.

Ultimately, she took the job and has had an amazing career thus far at Spotify. Did we have to scramble a bit to backfill her work? Yes, but we were able to anticipate the transition well in advance of her departure. And because of the mutual care and trust, Nicole continued to help us with some project work even after her last "official" day with us.

Our organization was and is better because of the eight months Nicole was with us. Other employees have joined Econic as direct referrals from Nicole. The story of Nicole and her Spotify job has become a bit of Econic cultural lore, which has helped make it safe for others to feel they can have collaborative, trust-first conversations with me or other leaders on our team about opportunities they might be considering.

Business goals are important. And so is the growth of the people who have chosen to be on our teams. In my naivete, I have chosen many times to prioritize the care and growth of those people *even over* business goals. That emphasis is key. Plenty of organizations focus on the care and growth of their people because they know it is a smart approach to achieving their business goals. I definitely applaud those organizations, especially over those who act more as if people are a resource to be maximized or even exploited in the pursuit of (often) financial gains.

But I want to challenge even the idea that growing people is the *means* to achieving profitable business *ends*. What if the *end* was the care and growth of the people that surround you, period? That doesn't mean you throw out business goals or financial targets; these can still be good things, and running a profitable business is necessary to *create* more opportunities for the care and growth of employees, customers, communities, and the planet. But what does it look like when you prioritize people *even over* business goals? Let's take a look at this through the eyes of another manager, Michael.

YOU > MY GOALS

"I'd like you to have coffee with Brad who works at the competitor down the street."

When the words came out of Michael's mouth, David was a bit stunned. He knew his boss was aware that this particular competitor was actively trying to recruit him. He was an outstanding employee, and both he and Michael knew that if he left, their company would be in a bind. And yet, he wasn't completely shocked. He knew Michael cared deeply about his development—even if it meant leaving his own team to pursue growth elsewhere.

In the traditional game of business, knowingly sending a star employee to meet with a competitor would be foolish. As a department leader at a fast-growing engineering firm, Michael is rewriting some of the rules of business and is more interested in playing the long game. A game he calls "mutual flourishing."

Michael knew his team member was going through a transition. After spending most of his career at the firm, David was questioning what else there might be in life. Michael had been a great leader for him and was still actively finding new responsibilities and projects for his growth, but David still wasn't content. Michael proactively began to identify other mentors who might be able to give David perspective on the next phase of life, both personally and professionally. One of those mentors just happened to work at their biggest competitor.

> I figure, two things can happen: (1) David learns something that enlightens him, and he chooses to go somewhere else. I'd miss a friend, and our team would be in a pickle. But I know he'd be doing what he thought was right for him, and I can put my head on the pillow at night being okay with that. Plus, it creates an opportunity internally for someone else to step up. Or (2) David learns some things and stays.

> We get better because of what he learns, and he knows that
> I actually did care enough to take that risk.

As you listen to Michael, you get the sense he feels like he wins either way. He's not ignoring risks, but he's more open to doing an "opportunity assessment" than a "risk assessment." In reality, he doesn't even see it as winning or losing. That's a zero-sum game, and Michael isn't interested in living that way. "I'm more interested in how a rising tide raises all boats"— mutual flourishing.

Behavior like Michael's also makes good business sense. In a recent study of more than 12,000 professionals, research found that "employees who say they have more supportive supervisors are 1.3 times as likely to stay with the organization and are 67 percent more engaged." Gallup found similar results: "Employees who report that their leader actively cares about their well-being are 81 percent less likely to seek a new employer in the next year and 41 percent less likely to miss work due to poor health."

In talking with Michael, though, you don't hear about percentages and statistics. You hear comments about legacy and how his faith fuels a more abundant and generous approach— an approach where business is important, but the growth of the individual is even more important. Again, this is what Michael would call the long game. "At my retirement party, I want to be surrounded by a bunch of people that are wildly successful in their specific interest or specific skill sets. Not because of something I specifically did for them, but because of how I cared about them and was an advocate for their opportunities."

What do you think? Can you hold the growth and development of employees even above the traditional growth goals of the company? Are these ideas mutually exclusive? When might this approach actually be damaging to the company or even the individual?

DARE TO BE NAIVE

Let's apply the reflection questions.

Let's take this through our reflection questions. Remember, this is about exploring perspectives, not about convincing you one way is right over another.

Caring for the growth of your employees is good for business.

If an employee's goal and a company goal conflict, the company goal should be prioritized.

If your employees are engaged and growing, then the business has a shot at growing.

Too many resources are spent on trying to accommodate every person's growth goals.

(Something else you come up with!)

Got a belief statement? Wonderful. Now, reflect on the stories as well as your well-earned life experience and answer the questions.

Where did I learn this belief?

_____

_____

_____

_____

Is this belief absolutely true?

_____

_____

_____

_____

What do I gain or would I gain by holding this belief?

_____

_____

_____

_____

What do I lose or would I lose by holding this belief?

_____

_____

_____

_____

Chapter 15

Rethinking Capitalism: Changing Lives through Creating Jobs, Not Charity

The sun was beating down. Sweat dripped from their brows. Dirty and exhausted, the workers realized they had a long way to go on this new building being constructed in northern Peru. They leaned on their shovels for a quick break. Yet, they couldn't quit because there were still a few more trenches to dig that day.

Seeing this pause in action, the engineering supervisor, conspicuously better dressed and absent of sweat, marched over to the workers. Fresh from earning his university degree and recently arrived from the capital city, Lima, he proceeded to berate the workers for their laziness. His words were hotter and more unforgiving than the blazing sun.

The crew was dejected. As the supervisor huffed away, one person spoke up. True, he was digging trenches like the rest of them, but you'd be hard pressed to call him a "local work-er." Andrew Vrbas, a nineteen-year-old farm boy from Kansas, had only been in the country for a year but had befriended this group of workers and was helping them out with their town projects as if he were a part of their community.

Andrew looked at the dejected workers and asked, "That guy seems to be a jerk; why don't you just quit?"

Unsuccessfully dabbing his forehead with an already soaked rag, one worker replied: "We can't quit. We're getting paid seven dollars a day, and we need to feed our families. This is the best job we can find here."

As Andrew recounted this story to me, he said, "And then, in typical American arrogance and naivete, I thought, 'I'm going to start something else to help these people.'" The year was 2010, and the spark for Pacha Soap was lit. The desire to serve others and use business for good, though, had been planted in Andrew generations prior.

In the early 1960s, Andrew's great-aunt Marian became one of the first Peace Corps volunteers. Established by newly elected President John F. Kennedy in the first months of his administration, the Peace Corps challenged citizens to "serve their country and the cause of peace by living and working in the developing world." Great-aunt Marian served in Peru.

During Marian's time there, her niece came to visit at age fifteen and felt it was a transformational experience. Not only did it inspire a servant's heart in her, but they developed many Peruvian family friends. Later, that niece, Kathy, would birth Andrew Vrbas, who at eighteen would be encouraged to visit one of those family friends in Peru.

By chance, Andrew was attending Hastings College at the time, which had a unique approach to allowing undergraduates the ability to configure their degrees. Andrew incorporated service and frequent trips to Peru into his college program, which is how he eventually found himself standing under the hot sun with some locals digging holes that day in 2010.

By literally working in the trenches of Peru, Andrew's thoughts evolved on ways to create better jobs for the locals. He also had some keen observations about sanitation and hygiene. During volunteer time at a local school, he saw the absence of running water and a hole in the ground for a bathroom. These were definitely sanitation and medical issues unthinkable in the modern world. In fact, Andrew recalled one student's dad died from constipation, of all things.

Out of these sanitation issues and the desire to create safer, better jobs, Andrew landed on the business of soapmaking. It did not require much equipment to get started. The skills were easy to teach. And the product was immediately beneficial to the developing communities. On top of that, Andrew felt like there might be a potential business opportunity to source local products and ingredients from these communities and bring them to the US market.

So why not just start a nonprofit? Andrew learned early in life on the family farm and from his father, a proud bricklayer, that there was dignity in work. One of the solutions to what he was seeing in these communities was to provide jobs—not charity. Around the same time as he started molding his idea for Pacha Soap, he observed the growing popularity of the TOMS Shoes One for One program. Started in 2006 and at the time deemed wildly successful, TOMS Shoes promised that for every pair of shoes that was purchased, another pair of shoes would be donated to a child who needed shoes in another country.

Andrew looked around at the kids he was seeing during his trips to Peru and imagined them all running around with pairs of TOMS shoes. The most common footwear for these kids were sandals made from recycled tires. Andrew questioned whether shoes made of fabric would actually *help* these kids (wet climate + fabric shoes + poor sanitation = foot diseases) *and* wondered what would happen to all the jobs of the local people who made the tire sandals. He vowed instead to approach any Pacha Soap give back program as an effort to grow people and jobs, not solely provide handouts. Ironically, by 2013, TOMS started to acknowledge some of the problems with their approach and drastically changed their One for One model, including moving to partnering with workers in local countries to provide the shoes intended for donation.

By 2016, Pacha Soap had donated one million bars of soap, and all of those bars had come from soapmaking businesses they helped establish within the countries from which they sourced materials. They've also established programs within countries to help locals develop fresh water initiatives and handwashing and sanitation classes for schools.

Today, Pacha Soap has over one hundred team members and is involved in forward-thinking approaches to using capitalism for good. Applying blockchain technology, they are implementing steps to ensure complete transparency and traceability in their supply chain as they strive to be leaders in what they are calling their "Farm to Bath" movement. They are also establishing new organic supplier partnerships with organizations like J-Palm Liberia. The joint mission is to boost income and empower small palm kernel and oil processors in Liberia, aiding five thousand farmers to create better opportunities for families in twenty rural communities. As Andrew shared with me during our time together, "In some parts of the world, small amounts of money change the narrative from losing children to saving children, from people going hungry to not."

Their successes in business have been recognized through various innovation and supplier awards from Whole Foods, a main partner with Pacha Soap and one of its largest retailers. While capitalism can sometimes get a bad rap, Andrew still feels it is one of the best structures to efficiently allocate capital and resources in a market. It's more about how you approach it. As Pacha Soap's 2021 Annual Impact Report proudly states, "We believe business can free people and that creating opportunity is better than creating charity. Our business is to empower people around the world with long-term sustainable solutions."

What do you think? Can business really *free* people? Is creating opportunity better than creating charity?

DARE TO BE NAIVE

Let's apply the reflection questions.

———————————————

Let's take one last pass through our reflection
questions. Choose a belief statement below that
resonates fully or partially with you or come up with
your own around this topic. Keep exploring new
perspectives!

*Business has the power to free people and set them
on a new trajectory.*

*Creating jobs and opportunities for people is
better than charity.*

*The idea that business can free people or meaningfully
change their lives is far-fetched.*

*Giving to charity is more effective and efficient
than creating jobs for people.*

(Something else you come up with!)

Got a belief statement? Great. Now, reflect on
Andrew's story as well as your well-earned life
experience and answer the questions.

Where did I learn this belief?

_____

_____

_____

_____

Is this belief absolutely true?

_____

_____

_____

_____

What do I gain or would I gain by holding this belief?

_____

_____

_____

_____

What do I lose or would I lose by holding this belief?

_____

_____

_____

_____

Chapter 16

Just Get Started

You have spent quite a bit of time creating space for yourself to be reflective in these previous chapters. I'm sure plenty of doubt crept in, and that's okay. The intent of this book was *not* to tell you all the things you're doing are wrong and try to convince you these practices and beliefs are superior. This is about learning, in general, how to adapt. Still, if you were able to keep an open mind to some concepts and challenging ideas, that attitude of curiosity is the first step in being able to adapt and evolve any new practices. This chapter will serve as a transition into what you can do with that attitude of curiosity.

There are three main things to consider as you focus on how you adapt: curiosity, action, and safety.

Curiosity is a desire to learn or know, often accompanied with a mindset of being open to something new or different. In general, I'm a curious person. Just today, I've been curious about a few things. When will my energy come back after my bout with COVID? How am I going to run this ethernet cable from my bedroom through the attic and into the basement? Will I ever get this popcorn hull dislodged from between these two molars? What will my editor think of this chapter? Sometimes I act on these curiosities (toothpick!), and other times, they don't make it past the curiosity stage. If you've been actively participating in this book, you're hopefully arriving at this chapter with a few curiosities of your own. You can choose to act on them, or not. It's your call. If you do choose to act on them, let's talk about that for a moment.

Action in this model refers to *any* action that puts part of that curiosity in motion. In fact, the bigger the curiosity, the smaller the resulting action needs to be to make progress (using that term lightly here) and keep the door open to another round of curiosity and action. If you're curious about trying something different, the biggest thing that often stops you from doing it is the fear of failing. Oftentimes, a smaller action is a safer action. If the smaller action leads to failure, it hurts less, especially if you take into account how you manage the third element, which is safety itself.

Safety in this model is anything that makes it easier, less scary, and more likely to complete another loop of curiosity and action. This can be the safety a manager provides on a team that makes it "safe to try" a new idea or share a minority opinion. It can be an actual personal state of physical, emotional, or mental well-being (or even just the perception) that allows you to feel like you can wonder, try, and then try again if needed.

Think of it like a child learning to walk. There is some impulse, some "I wonder if" that propels a child to try its first step. The child doesn't start off running. It takes a small action. And (often) the caregiver is there to provide some level of safety, with a hand to hold or some toy to help provide support.

Our kids all learned to walk with the help of a bubble mower. (They looked cute but did a terrible job mowing straight lines.) They of course fell down time and time again but were able to learn and keep adapting.

Let's take an example of one of the beliefs we explored in part 2 of the book: prioritizing people's growth even over short-term business outcomes. Let's say you were curious about how you might act on this idea. What's the smallest piece of action you could take to explore this curiosity? You don't have to immediately rewrite your employee handbook and the related policies in your organization. How about starting with a conversation with one of the best performers on your team? In your next coaching conversation, try working in one of the following questions:

- On a 1–10 scale, how much of "you" do you get to be at this job? If not a 10, what could be changed to get that closer to a 10?

- What's something you've always wanted to do, even if it isn't immediately apparent how it would benefit this company?

- If you weren't at this job, what would you be doing instead?

- What's a professional area you'd like to grow in?

  What's a personal area you'd like to grow in?

In this instance, you also have the responsibility of the safety part of the model. This whole exchange doesn't work if there is little trust between the two of you. If there is hesitation to share things that don't seem "company aligned," consider going first and sharing something you might change about your job. Bonus points if it is an area you want to grow in that might not seem readily apparent to benefit the organization. Appropriate vulnerability is a great bridge to trust.

THE MODEL IN ACTION

Jered is a senior leader at a large national engineering firm. As he's working with his teams, he prioritizes creating a sense of safety for them to authentically talk about their goals and aspirations. "At the end of the day, life is short, and business careers are even shorter. My life is going to be marked by how I've helped and served other people."

I was facilitating a strategic alignment workshop for Jered and his team when I got to see his beliefs about serving other people in action. While the primary purpose of the day was to discuss the direction of the team, he opened up the conversation asking the second question above: "What's something you've always wanted to do, even if it isn't immediately apparent how it would benefit this company?"

Jered created safety by leading off the conversation. He shared his desire to do more work with walkable, urban developments, maybe even starting his own company upon retirement. Team members followed suit and shared dreams like opening a clothing boutique, caddying in Scotland, and working from a catamaran half of the year. It was obvious the team felt comfortable sharing those things with their boss, and it was evident Jered cared about learning these things (which, of course, were in their minds whether he asked about it or not). With those dreams out on the table, it then became possible to talk about small ways that parts of those dreams might be achieved or even intertwined with the direction of the broader team.

YOUR ROLE

At any level in an organization, you have the power and "response-ability" to create a safe place for people to be curious and bravely try new things. By modeling curiosity, admitting mistakes, or withholding immediate judgment when people present ideas you disagree with, you will make it more likely that people will be able to learn new beliefs and practices. The ability to reflect on a central belief—especially one that is core to our identity—and consider "I might be wrong" is a sign of emerging or realized wisdom and maturity.

At the heart of it, you're helping people self-learn, iterate, and adapt. This adaptability is essential in a world that requires you and your organization to be even more change-ready than ever before. Why? Well let's dig into a metaphor Jean-François Zobrist, from chapter 5, used with people at FAVI. It has to do with understanding the difference between a *complicated* and a *complex* situation or system.

A car engine is a *complicated* system. There may be thousands of parts, but they all have a place and respond in a logical way. If you take out any one part, a skilled repairman could tell you if and how it would impact the engine. If the world, your organization, or even your life functioned exactly like a car engine, we could analyze, plan, and execute any needed changes with a high level of precision.

Unfortunately, we approach many challenges in life as if they were just complicated. You try to analyze, plan, and execute, and only rarely do plans turn out the way you predict. The problem is most systems in life are actually *complex*, not complicated. The ecosystem in your backyard, for instance, is *complex*. You can seek to understand all the different components involved in the system, but there is no possible way to 100 percent predict the outcome of one action on the system or another. Jean-François liked to use the image of a bowl of spaghetti to describe a complex system: "It has only a few dozen parts, but tug at one end of a strand of spaghetti that sticks out, and even the most powerful computer in the world will not be able to predict what will happen."

In a complex system, the best way to approach change is to iterate and adapt, sense and respond, and practice the loop of curiosity and action and create the safe environment for others to do the same.

Now, I want you to think about one of the ideas from the book that you're curious about—maybe even something others might say would be naive to act on, yet the most genuine, authentic part of you would consider it.

Is there any fear preventing you from acting on this belief? What would need to happen for you to have the safety to try something different or new, even at the smallest level? Author and leadership expert, Nicole Bianchi, calls this bravery with a lowercase *b*. Too often we think bravery is just saving someone from a burning building, yet "consistent, little acts of bravery" are essential to life-changing work. They are also key to moral excellence, as Aristotle pointed out: "We become just by doing just acts, temperate by doing temperate acts, brave by doing brave acts."

YOUR TURN

Fill in the following blanks:

I'm curious about_____.
The next small action I can take is_____.
I can enhance safety by_____.

One of my favorite activities to help navigate this last question of enhancing personal safety comes from author, podcast host, and entrepreneur-investor Tim Ferriss. We spend so much time goal-setting and planning for success—he suggests you also tackle "fear-setting." The beauty of this exercise is that we suffer most often in our imagination—not reality. The questions below help you name your fears and nightmares that might be holding you back from acting.

To start, we need to examine our fears. Instead of ignoring them, we put them under a microscope and really try to understand them more clearly.

Think of something you'd like to try but seems scary to consider. Now, grab a sheet of paper and do the following exercise.

Step 1: Make three columns and label them "Define," "Prevent," and "Repair."

Step 2: In column one, define everything you fear about taking action on the idea you selected.

List out your worst-case scenarios, your doubts, the big nightmare disaster. List all of your what-ifs. Write it all down, and don't hold back.

- What's the worst-case scenario?

- What might go wrong?

- On a 1–10 scale, with 1 being nothing and 10 being permanently disastrous and irrecoverable, what would you rate the impact of these worst-case scenarios?

Step 3: In column two, under "Prevent," list ways you could reduce the probability of each of the nightmare scenarios from happening.

What actions could you take to make those scenarios from column one less likely to happen?

Step 4: In column three, under "Repair," list ways you could repair the damage *if* the worst-case scenario were to *actually* come true.

What actions could you take to get yourself back on track?

DEFINE	PREVENT	REPAIR
WHAT'S THE WORST THAT COULD HAPPEN? GET SPECIFIC RATE 1-10	WHAT SPECIFICALLY COULD YOU DO TO REDUCE THE CHANCE OF THESE SITUATIONS HAPPENING?	IF IT DOES HAPPEN, WHAT COULD YOU DO TO GET BACK ON TRACK?

I'll provide an example, using an idea from one of Jered's team members above. Here's what it might look like for the person who was dreaming about starting a clothing boutique.

Although there's only a couple fears illustrated below, add as many as you can when you do your own exercise.

EXAMPLE: LEAVE JOB, START CLOTHING BOUTIQUE

DEFINE	PREVENT	REPAIR
IT WON'T BE SUCCESSFUL, I'LL RUN OUT OF MONEY AND HAVE TO SELL MY HOUSE - 6 I'LL BURN A BRIDGE WITH MY BOSS AND WON'T BE ABLE TO RETURN TO WORK HERE - 3 IT'LL TAKE MORE TIME THAN I HAVE, AND I WON'T HAVE TIME FOR MY KIDS WHO WILL RESENT ME - 5	• REDUCE COSTS OF LIVING • WORK WITH STARTUP COACH • START WITH A POP-UP STORE • BE OPEN WITH BOSS ABOUT IDEA • DELIVER GREAT WORK UNTIL LAST DAY • NEGOTIATE PART-TIME ROLE • FIND A PARTNER • BE OPEN WITH MY KIDS ABOUT THE DREAM	• GO BACK TO FORMER EMPLOYER • RENT OUT PART OF HOUSE • APPLY FOR A JOB • NETWORK AND START APPLYING FOR OTHER JOBS • HELP KIDS SEE THAT IT'S OKAY TO TRY • BRING KIDS INTO AGE-APPROPRIATE DECISIONS

Filling out the table in this exercise will put into perspective the pros and cons of your ideas. Very often, you'll see that it is easier and less scary than you thought to just get started. If you do the exercise (and you made it this far in the book!), drop me a note at joshua@econic.co and let me know how it went for you or what questions you still have. I can also share some additional ways to put your ideas into action.

YOUR RIPPLE OF IMPACT

As Chip Conley shared in chapter 7, "When you drop a pebble in a pond, it creates a series of ripples that cascade out over the water. . . . The choices we make on where we purchase, how we build our company culture, and how we affect our community make a profound difference—sending energy into the world that will create positive or negative ripples." The power to do more good in your life, in your organization, or on your team starts with you. We need *you* to create positive Ripples of Impact.

Make time to consider newer and more conscious ways of leading people, growing business, or interacting with the marketplace. And when you come up with an idea that sounds too optimistic or idealistic, pause before you quiet that inner voice. Remember that naive inner voice represents something more innate, genuine, and authentic than the world often appreciates.

The world has enough people already thinking we're doomed or it's too late, too many people standing on the sidelines because their noblest ideas are outside of the mainstream.

It's going to take brave, naive people like you to act on the brighter future you can envision and that others may think is impossible.

Dare to be naive.

Acknowledgments

This book was inspired by a small voice inside that has a big vision for the evolution of the workplace and education. If we evolve the concepts, systems, and cultures of work and school, more human potential on the world's biggest problems can be unleashed. As I dug deeper into why more leaders were not embracing stakeholder capitalism, 1% for the Planet, Benefit Corporations, etc., it became clear that it wasn't for lack of how-to books or case studies. At the core, it kept coming back to the need for leaders to have greater shifts in consciousness, awareness, and belief. This book is my naive attempt at encouraging some of those shifts.

Over the years, I've been asked many times when I would write a book, and typically I said I wouldn't. "There are already plenty of books," I would retort. "I'm a curator, not a creator."

I still believe there are already plenty of books. However, in fall of 2021, I discovered this was just an excuse I was telling myself to avoid the fear of rejection, the fear of claiming an idea and putting it in writing for people to love, hate, and everything in between. I am grateful to my purpose guide Niharika Sanyal and my great friend and enneagram coach Jon Kohrs for helping me with this area of growth. Without you, this book would not have manifested itself through me (yet).

Thank you to my best friend and life partner, Trisha Lynn. Thank you for the support and time to write, but more importantly, thank you for the encouragement, safety, and space for me to be naive. You are a selfless and cheerful giver, unmatched in the world. I cherish the life we're experiencing together, and I love you forever and ever, and a little bit longer than that.

Thank you to my children, Chloe, Logan, Gavin, and Daphne. Thank you for your patience the past year as I poured evening, weekend, and in-between hours into this book. I appreciate how you invite me in so many ways to pause and rediscover my childlike wonder and naivete. I love you all deeply.

To my dad, Jerry, thank you for always thinking bigger. You've passed that on to me and always worked hard to provide the best for us. Your grit and resilience are admirable. I would not be who I am today without you, and I love you.

To my mom, Jolene, thank you for creating the security I needed to flourish amid years of instability. It is in complexity that we have the chance to grow the most. I had the opportunity to grow and thrive because of the order and love you provided. I would not be who I am today without you, and I love you.

Thank you to my coach, cheerleader, confidant, and dear friend Diana Kander. First off, thank you for the charity auction package that got me into the Manuscripts LLC writer's program. Nobody would be reading these words if not for you. Thank you for the honest feedback and creative brainstorming throughout this journey. I appreciate all the dreaming, experimenting, and support these last several years.

Thank you to the team at Econic. I appreciate your time, space, and encouragement over the past year to work on this book. Thank you for serving our clients in such a heart-centered, impact-oriented way. I am better because of each of you. A special thank you to Julie Wilbeck, Brittany Bach, and Maddy Fredrick for your work on edits and marketing. And to Krystal Wiebelhaus—the "CEO of this book launch"—I can't put into words how grateful I am that you came back into my life at this exact time to help bring this into the world. You are a dynamo.

Thank you to the magnanimous leaders who inspired and were interviewed for this book. Jeff Cherry and Chip Conley—your past and current support are life-giving, I am constantly inspired by your work. Manisha Singh—you are powerful in so many ways. Aric Wood, Doug Waltman, Jered Morris, Michael Bash, Nicole Shephard, Brian Ardinger, Colin Robertson, Evan Roth, James Murphy, Craig Moody, Andrew Vrbas, Daniel Lawse, Heidi Harsin—thank you for your time, talent, and stories. And Craig Clasen—my intro chapter Hy-Vee hero, thanks for believing in me. Rest assured, I didn't include the story of when you ran over my foot with a forklift . . . until now.

One of my greatest sources of inspiration for this work is the book *The Healing Organization* by Raj Sisodia and Michael Gelb. Please go read that book next if you haven't already. Thank you, Raj, for the work you are doing in this movement and for making time to help me along this journey.

Thank you to the many early beta readers, both new and old friends from all walks of my life. A special measure of gratitude goes to Scott Focht, Fred Hockett, and Jaime Baim Hansen for reviewing extra chapters. Jordan Birnbaum, you "got" my voice and helped me with many pivotal edits midway through this journey—thank you!

I have deep appreciation for the following people who supported me and this book through preorders and participation in my online Author's Community. They helped make this book possible, from ideating on the final title and book cover to constant support and encouragement. Your votes of confidence meant the world to me and helped me stand a little taller.

Maisah Ali, Dan Arnold, Danielle Bayer (Hill), Adam Berk, Jason Berry, Jolene Berry, Nicole Bianchi, Blake Birkel, Jeremy Bouman, Beth Bruss, Kara Bunde-Dunn, Denise Caleb, Jared Carlson, Kyle Cartwright, Peggy Christensen, Allison Dahl, Bart Dillashaw, Eric Dinger, Astrid Doerner, Abby Donnelly, Dee Drozd, Bill Eckstrom, Casee Eisele, Scott Focht, Ben Fogle, Chris Fox, Peter Grenier, Cali Harris, Steve Hawkins, Karen Helmberger, Richard Herrick, Katie Hertel, Patrick Hodge, Steve Ingracia, Blake Johnston, Tim Kiefer, Eric Koester, Jon Kohrs, Liz Koop, Brent Korte, Valerie Lancelle, Eunice Lee, Bill Lester, Megan Lilley, Cameron Ludwig, Katie Mach, Austin Mackrill, Niki Manby, Brady Marlow, Erica McClurg, Lora Miller, Eric Mooss, Jason Muhleisen, Colin Mulholland, Melissa Newton, Anna Novotny, Boyd Ober, Bridgett Ojeda, Sandro Olivieri, Amy Ostermeyer, Graham Pansing Brooks, Patrick Patterson, Ryan Pavel, Matt Poepsel, Brian Poppe,

McKell Purnell, Ramya Ramaswamy, Dave Rippe, Liz Robertson, Colin Robertson, Marissa Rodgerson, Evan Roth, Steph Schott, Ali Schwanke, Bryan Seck, Jeff Shannon, Evan Sheaff, Cassandra Smalley, Pawel Smolarkiewicz, Jessie Sprotte, Larry Sternberg, Katie Thompson, Matthew Vander Laan, Daniel Volk, Andrew Vrbas, Cami Wacker, Brad Walton, Alan Wang, Gary Warren, DeeAnn Wenger, Joel Weyand, Nathan Wildauer, Jay Wilkinson, Nancy Williams, Philip Zeccardi, and Dixie Ziegler.

Thank you to Eric Koester, John Saunders, and the team at Manuscripts LLC for flipping my idea of writing a book on its head. You made this seem possible and then helped make it so. Thanks to Lucas Click for early editing and cheerleading. Special thanks to Ilia Epifanov, my amazing revisions editor who drastically improved the book and shares my romantic, idealistic view of the world. I appreciate you, my friend.

Thank you to the team at Ideapress Publishing, including Rohit Bhargava, Chhavi Bhargava, Marnie McMahon, Kameron Bryant-Sergejev, Megan Wheeler, and Jessica Angerstein.

Thank you to Emily Willette, Olivia McCoy, Macy Mohr, Katie Ferraro, Kellie Rendina, Erin MacDonald-Birnbaum, and the rest of the team at Smith Publicity for amplifying my naive voice in the world.

Thank you to Amber Vilhauer, Lauren Erickson, Courtney Cook, Cierra Warner, and all of the team behind the scenes at NGNG Enterprises for your help with the book launch strategy, website, personal branding, and for just being amazing, authentic, caring people.

And finally, thank you for reading this book. Investing in your own growth is priceless; may what is for the highest good and benefit of all happen because of it.

References

INTRODUCTION

Fink, Larry. 2018. "Larry Fink's 2018 Letter to CEOs: A Sense of Purpose." BlackRock. https://www.blackrock.com/corporate/investor-relations/2018-larry-fink-ceo-letter.

PricewaterhouseCoopers, LLP. 2015. "Make It Your Business: Engaging with the Sustainable Development Goals." https://www.pwc.com/gx/en/sustainability/SDG/SDG%20Research_FINAL.pdf.

CHAPTER 1—NAIVE: A FRESH TAKE ON AN OLD WORD

Aberystwyth University. 2014. "Word of the Month: Nice! An Anglo-Norman Insult." *Anglo-Norman Dictionary*. https://anglo-norman.net/word-of-the-month-nice-an-anglo-norman-insult/.

Friedman, Jacob. 2021. "Hayden and the Aesthetics of Naivety." *Music and Letters* 102, no. 4 (September): 687–718. https://doi.org/10.1093/ml/gcab063.

Firestone, Lisa. 2012. "Is Cynicism Ruining Your Life?" *Psychology Today*, December 2012. https://www.psychologytoday.com/us/blog/

compassion-matters/201212/is-cynicism- ruining-your-life/.

Hill, Jemele. 2010. "Under Armour's Kevin Plank Talks Shop." ESPN. http://www.espn.com/espn/page2/story?sport-Cat=ncf&id=4846753.

Jaipur Rugs Company Pvt. Ltd. 2022. Jaipur Rugs. https://www.jaipurrugs.com/us/about/company.

LMN Technology Pvt. Ltd. 2022. "Anatole France Quotes." Allauthor. https://allauthor.com/quotes/93532/.

O'Reilly, Barry. 2018. *Unlearn: Let Go of Past Success to Achieve Extraordinary Results*. New York: McGraw Hill.

Rohr, Richard. 2011. *Falling Upward: A Spirituality for the Two Halves of Life*. San Francisco: Jossey-Bass.

Schultz, Howard. 2008. "Talking with the King of Coffee." Interviewed by Katie Couric. CBS Evening News with Katie Couric. December 8, 2008.

Sisodia, Raj, and Michael J. Gelb. 2019. *The Healing Organization: Awakening the Conscience of Business to Help Save the World*. Nashville: HarperCollins Leadership.

Speake, Jennifer, and Mark LaFlaur. 2002. *The Oxford Essential Dictionary of Foreign Terms in English*. Oxford Reference. 1st ed. New York: Oxford University Press. https://www.oxfordreference.com/view/10.1093/acref/9780199891573.001.0001/acref- 9780199891573-e-4616.

Tufts University. n.d. "Charlton T. Lewis, *An Elementary Latin Dictionary*." Perseus Digital Library. Accessed August 14, 2022. http://www.perseus.tufts.edu/hopper/ text?doc=Perseus:text-t:1999.04.0060:entry=nativus.

CHAPTER 2—THE AUTHENTIC, UNCONVENTIONAL, AND INTENTIONAL YVON CHOUINARD

1% for the Planet. 2020. "Putting People and Planet Over Profit." One Percent for the Planet. https://www.onepercentfortheplanet. org/.

B Lab. 2022. "Building the Movement." B Corporation. https://www. bcorporation.net/en-us/movement.

Chouinard, Yvon. 2006. *Let My People Go Surfing: The Education of a Reluctant Businessman*. New York: Penguin.

Chouinard, Yvon, and Tom Frost. 1972. "A word . . ." *1972 Chouinard Mountain Climbing Equipment Catalog*. January 1972. https://climbaz.com/chouinard72/ch_page2.html.

Gelles, David. 2022. "Billionaire No More: Patagonia Founder Gives Away the Company." *New York Times*. September 14, 2022. https:// www.nytimes.com/2022/09/14/climate/patagonia-climate-philan-thropy-chouinard.html.

Fat Buddha Store. n.d. "Patagonia Brand Timeline." Fat Buddha Store. Accessed August 17, 2022. https://www.fatbuddhastore.com/ patagonia-timeline-i278.

Leighton, Mara. 2019. "8 Popular Companies like Nike and Patago-nia That Are Committed to Reducing Environmental Harm by Using Organic Cotton." *Insider*. Accessed August 17, 2022. https://www. insider.com/guides/style/sustainable-organic-cotton-clothes- bed-ding-2019-1.

Patagonia, Inc. 2022. "Fair Trade." Patagonia. https://www.patago-nia.com/our-footprint/fair-trade.html.

CHAPTER 3—RIPPLES OF IMPACT AND THE POWER OF BELIEFS

Jung, C. G. 1979. *Aion: Researches into the Phenomenology of the Self.* Princeton, N.J.: Princeton University Press.

Kahneman, Daniel. 2011. *Thinking, Fast and Slow.* New York: Farrar, Straus and Giroux.

Kofman, Fred. "Response-ability." *Creations Magazine.* February/March 2007. http://www.creationsmagazine.com/articles/C112/Kofman.html.

Kofman, Fred. 2006. *Conscious Business: How to Build Value Through Values.* Boulder, Colorado: Sounds True.

CHAPTER 4—EVOLVING YOUR BELIEFS: A PROFOUND YET SIMPLE APPROACH

Agarwal, Pragya. "Understanding Unconscious Bias." Interview with Emily Kwong.

NPR Short Wave. Podcast audio. July 15, 2020. https://www.npr.org/2020/07/14/891140598/understanding-unconscious-bias.

Bermingham, Kevin. 2010. *Change Your Limiting Beliefs: Three Steps to Achieve Meaningful Goals.* Sussex: Meaningful Goals, Ltd.

George E. P. Box. "Science and Statistics." *Journal of the American Statistical Association* 71, no. 356 (1976): 791–99. https://doi.org/10.2307/2286841.

Godin, Seth. 2022. "The Win-Win Fallacy." *Seth's Blog* (blog). April 24, 2022. https://seths.blog/2022/04/the-win-win-fallacy/.

Jung, C. G. 1978. *Psychology and the East: (From Vols. 10, 11, 13, 18 Collected Works).* Princeton: Princeton University Press.

Katie, Byron. 2016. *Loving What Is: Four Questions That Can Change Your Life.* Read by Byron Katie. New York: Random House Audio. Audible audio ed., 9hr., 7 min.

Levitan, Daniel J. 2015. "Why It's So Hard to Pay Attention, Explained by Science." *Fast Company*. September 2015. https://www.fastcompany.com/3051417/why-its-so-hard-to-pay-attention-explained-by-science.

Schneider, Bruce D. 2022. *Energy Leadership: The 7 Level Framework for Mastery in Life and Business*. 2nd ed. Hoboken, New Jersey: Wiley.

Toffler, Alvin. 1970. *Future Shock*. New York: Random House.

CHAPTER 5—UNLOCKING TOOLS: HOW A NAIVE, LAZY BOSS LIBERATED A FACTORY

Minnaar, Joost. 2017. "FAVI: How Zobrist Broke Down FAVI's Command-and-Control Structures." Corporate Rebels. https://corporate-rebels.com/zobrist/.

Laloux, Frederic. 2014. *Reinventing Organizations: A Guide to Creating Organizations Inspired by the Next Stage in Human Consciousness*. 1st edition. Brussels: Nelson Parker.

Minnaar, Joost. 2017. "FAVI: How Giving Freedom to Factory Workers Created Massive Success." Corporate Rebels. https://corporate-rebels.com/favi-part-2/.

Taylor, Frederick Winslow. 1926. Testimony of Frederick W. Taylor at Hearings before Special Committee of the House of Representatives, January 1912. New York.

Zobrist, Jean-François. 2014. *La belle histoire de Favi : l'entreprise qui croit que l'homme est bon Tome 1 Nos belles histoires*. Paris: HUMANISME & ORGANISATIONS.

Zobrist, Jean-François. 2020. *L'entreprise libérée par le petit patron naïf et paresseux*. Paris: Cherche Midi.

CHAPTER 6—INSPIRED ENGINEERING: DESIGNING LOVE INTO ALGORITHMS AND AI

Economic History Organization. n.d. "History of Workplace Safety in the United States, 1880–1970." EH. Accessed September 27, 2022. https://eh.net/encyclopedia/history-of-workplace-safety-in-the-united-states-1880-1970-2/.

Tata Sons Private Limited. 2019-2022. "People First." Tata. https://www.tata.com/newsroom/people-first-labour-welfare.

CHAPTER 7—GIVING MORE: A HOTELIER'S APPROACH TO KARMIC CAPITALISM

Conley, Chip. 2007. *Peak: How Great Companies Get Their Mojo from Maslow*. San Francisco: Jossey-Bass.

Conley, Chip. 2021. "Ripples of Impact: A New Form of ROI." *Wisdom Well* (blog), Modern Elder Academy. October 17, 2021. https://wisdomwell.modernelderacademy.com/.

Ferriss, Tim. "#374: Chip Conley—Building Empires, Tackling Cancer, and Surfing the Liminal." *The Tim Ferriss Show*. Podcast. June 2019. 1:53. https://open.spotify.com/episode/11XUxz9rDp2qeVoEwd-FERSsi=whuwrgJESZeYFJmG_3JAvw&nd=1.

GiveWell. 2022. "Against Malaria Foundation." https://www.givewell.org/charities/amf.

MacAskill, William. 2015. *Doing Good Better: Effective Altruism and a Radical New Way to Make a Difference*. New York: Avery.

Strauss, Robert L. 2001. "The Karmic Capitalism of Chip Conley." *Stanford Magazine*. September/October 2001. https://stanfordmag.org/contents/the-karmic-capitalism-of-chip-conley.

The Centre for Effective Altruism. n.d. "What Is Effective Altruism?" Effective Altruism. Accessed September 21, 2022. https://www.effectivealtruism.org/articles/introduction-to-effective-altruism.

Todd, Benjamin. 2020. "Misconceptions about Effective Altruism." *80,000 Hours* (blog). August 7, 2020. https://80000hours. org/2020/08/misconceptions-effective-altruism/.

CHAPTER 8—SIDE HUSTLES: ENCOURAGING WORK BEYOND THE JOB

Costa, MaryLou. 2021. "'Your Career Doesn't Have to Be Your Entire Life': Why Some Companies Are Encouraging Side Hustles." Worklife. https://www.worklife.news/Culture/your-career-doesnt-have-to-be-your-entire-life- why-some-companies-are-encouraging-side-hustles/.

Handley, Lucy. 2021. "'I Can't Believe You're Allowed to Do That': Meet the Companies Encouraging Side Hustles." CNBC Work. https://www.cnbc.com/2021/12/22/these-companies-actually-encourage-staff-to- have-side-hustles.html.

Marcot, April. 2020. "How to Manage Outcomes, Not Hours." *Talent International* (blog). March 2020. https://www.talentinternational. us/blog/2020/03/how-to-manage-outcomes-not-hours.

Whitter, Ben. 2021. *Human Experience at Work: Drive Performance with a People-Focused Approach to Employees*. London: Kogan.

CHAPTER 9—DEPLOYING CONSCIOUS CAPITAL: A REMIX OF BUSINESS AND LEADERSHIP JAZZ

Cherry, Jeff. "Damon Lawrence." *Capitalism: The Remix*. Podcast. March 10, 2022. 37:01. https://capitalismtheremix.podbean.com/e/capitalism-the-remix-damon-lawrence/.

Cone Communications. 2016. "Millennial Employee Engagement Study." https://static1.squarespace.com/static/56b4a7472b8dde3df5b-7013f/t/5819e8b303596e301 6ca0d9c/1478092981243/2016+Cone+Communications+Millennial+Employee+Engagem ent+Study_Press+Release+and+Fact+Sheet.pdf.

Conscious Capitalism, Inc. 2021. "Conscious Capitalism." https://www.consciouscapitalism.org/.

De Pree, Max. 2008. *Leadership Jazz—Revised Edition: The Essential Elements of a Great Leader.* New York: Doubleday.

Gold Standard. 2018. "Business and the Sustainable Development Goals: Best Practices to Seize Opportunity and Maximize Credibility." SDG Report. https://www.goldstandard.org/sites/default/files/documents/sdg_report_optimized.pdf.

Harter, Jim. 2021. "U.S. Employee Engagement Data Hold Steady in First Half of 2021." Gallup. July 2021. https://www.gallup.com/workplace/352949/employee-engagement-holds-steady-first- half-2021.aspx.

Mackey, John, and Rajendra Sisodia. 2013. *Conscious Capitalism: Liberating the Heroic Spirit of Business.* Boston: Harvard Business Review Press.

CHAPTER 10—SHARING IDEAS: LOOSENING THE GRIP ON IP AND TRADE SECRETS

APB Speakers. 2015. "Patrick Lencioni: The Ultimate Competitive Advantage: Why Organizational Health Trumps Everything Else." YouTube. January 6, 2015. 1:23. https://www.youtube.com/watch?v=HxjFQ3y0M6I.

Carr, Austin. 2013. "Deep Inside Taco Bell's Doritos Locos Tacos." *Fast Company*. https://www.fastcompany.com/3008346/deep-inside-taco-bells-doritos-locos-taco.

CBS News. 2012. "Big Mac Special Sauce: Chef Shows How It's Made." YouTube. July 11, 2012. 0:56. https://www.youtube.com/watch?v=c4QOHBuloG8.

GitHub, Inc. 2022. "GitHub." Accessed September 2, 2022. https:// github.com/.

Lencioni, Patrick. 2012. *The Advantage*. San Francisco: Jossey-Bass.

Makalintal, Bettina. 2020. "Brands Are Giving Away Their Secret Recipes because of Coronavirus." *Vice*. April 2020. https://www.vice.com/en/article/7kzynq/brands-are-giving-away-their-secret- recipes-because-of-coronavirus.

Musk, Elon. 2013. "Hyperloop Alpha." White Paper. https://www. tesla.com/sites/default/files/blog_images/hyperloop-alpha.pdf.

Williams, Jordan. 2020. "Bend Soup Company." YouTube. April 9, 2020. 1:39. http://ktvz.com/news/2020/04/09/bend-soup-compa-ny-releasing-secret-recipes-to-public/.

CHAPTER 11—UNCONVENTIONAL PURPOSE: USING FOR-PROFIT AS A MEANS TO A DIFFERENT END

Chapman, Bob, and Rajendra Sisodia. 2015. *Everybody Matters: The Extraordinary Power of Caring for Your People Like Family*. New York: Portfolio/Penguin.

Rivard, Robert. 2018. "Charles Butt Take the Giving Pledge: 'It's the Right Thing to Do'." *San Antonio Report*. June 9, 2018. https://sanantonioreport.org/charles-butt-takes-the-pledge-its-the-right-thing-to-do/.

Sisodia, Rajendra, and Michael J. Gelb. 2019. *Awakening the Conscience of Business to Help Save the World*. Nashville: HarperCollins Leadership.

CHAPTER 12—TRUST TRANSACTIONS: LESSONS FROM PAY-WHAT-YOU-WANT BUSINESSES

Blanding, Michael. 2015. "Pay What You Wish: What Happens When Customers Choose the Price." *Forbes*. July 2015. https://www.forbes.com/sites/hbsworkingknowledge/2015/07/22/pay-whatever-you-want-when-retailers-let-customers-name-their-price/?sh=3f9d98e-91ae0.

Dewaan, Natalie. 2015. "This Pakistani Restaurant in Vienna Runs on Trust." Interviewed by Kiran Haroon. *Dawn*. May 7, 2015. https://www.dawn.com/news/1180531. (Accessed September 2, 2022).

Kim, Ju-Young, Martin Natter, and Martin Spann. 2009. "Pay What You Want: A New Participative Pricing Mechanism." *Journal of Marketing* 73, no. 1 (January): 44-58. https://www.ecm.bwl.uni-muenchen.de/publikationen/pdf/pwyw_jm.pdf.

Peters, Adele. 2018. "Why Panera's Experiment with Pay-What-You-Want Dining Failed." *Fast Company*. June 2018. https://www.fastcompany.com/40582757/why-paneras-experiment-with-pay-what-you-want-dining-failed.

CHAPTER 13—BEING INTENTIONAL: CHALLENGING GROWTH FOR GROWTH'S SAKE

Burlingham, Bo. 2016. *Small Giants: Companies That Choose to Be Great Instead of Big, 10th Anniversary Edition*. London: Portfolio.

Chouinard, Yvon. 2006. *Let My People Go Surfing: The Education of a Reluctant Businessman*. New York: Penguin.

Collins, Jim. 2009. *How the Mighty Fall: And Why Some Companies Never Give In*. Boulder: HarperCollins.

CHAPTER 14—PEOPLE FIRST: PRIORITIZING EMPLOYEE GROWTH EVEN OVER THE COMPANY'S

Gabsa, Robert, and Shruti Rastogi. 2020. "Take Care of Your People, and They'll Take Care of Business." Gallup. June 23, 2020. https://www.gallup.com/workplace/312824/care-people-care-business.aspx.

Schwartz, Tony, and Christine Porath. 2014. "The Power of Meeting Your Employees' Needs." *Harvard Business Review*. June 30, 2014. https://hbr.org/2014/06/the-power-of-meeting-your-employees-needs.

CHAPTER 15—RETHINKING CAPITALISM: CHANGING LIVES THROUGH CREATING JOBS, NOT CHARITY

Hessekiel, David. 2021. "The Rise and Fall of the Buy-One-Give-One Model at TOMS." *Forbes*. April 2021. https://www.forbes.com/sites/davidhessekiel/2021/04/28/the-rise-and-fall-of-the- buy-one-give-one-model-at-toms/?sh=b2f648371c45.

Pacha Soap Company. 2021. "Pacha Soap Co: Raising the Bar." Annual Report. https://indd.adobe.com/view/168677a2-6c88-44b9-85ea-6bee05444540.

CHAPTER 16—JUST GET STARTED

Aristotle, David Ross, and Lesley Brown. 2009. *The Nicomachean Ethics*. Oxford and New York: Oxford University Press.

Bianchi, Nicole M. 2021. *Small Brave Moves: Learn Why Little Acts of Bravery Are the Key to Life-Changing Leadership*. Washington, DC: New Degree Press.

Ferriss, Tim. "Fear-Setting: The Most Valuable Exercise I Do Every Month." *The Tim Ferriss Show*. Podcast. May 15, 2017. 13:12. https://tim.blog/2017/05/15/fear-setting.

Laloux, Frederic. 2014. *Reinventing Organizations: A Guide to Creating Organizations Inspired by the Next Stage in Human Consciousness.* 1st edition. Brussels: Nelson Parker.

Zobrist, Jean-François. 2020. *L'entreprise libérée par le petit patron naïf et paresseux.* Paris: Cherche Midi.